OUR FUTURE, OUR PLANET, AND US

Betty Gelinas

ISBN -10:1503204847

ISBN -13:978-1503204843

Cover Graphic and Design: Mary Willoughby
                                           David Fournier

Dedicated to Planet Earth

Many thanks and appreciation to my family and friends for their help and encouragement throughout this process.

CONTENTS

PART I

INTRODUCTION

OUR EARTH

While most of us have seen pictures of our blue and white planet as it moves serenely through the blackness of space, it's strange that so lovely a sight should hold on its surface millions of suffering human beings and vast areas of destruction. It should be as beautiful below as it appears to be from above.

In his book *The Hidden Face Of God*, nuclear physicist Gerald Schroeder writes:

> "We are, each of us, a part of the universe seeking itself…Every particle, every being, from atom to human appears to have within it a level of information, of conscious wisdom."[1]

Referring to this conscious wisdom residing in our minds as the *Neshama*, Schroeder explains that even though it always knows if our thoughts unite us or keep us apart, it "can act only on the choices with which it is presented."[2]

In other words it must and will follow the direction of our thoughts. And just as we can't see, touch, or smell the force of gravity, neither can we see, touch, or smell the force of our thoughts. Yet, these two forces are equally as powerful. Everything we see on our planet was first a thought.

Introduction

[1]Gerald L. Schroeder. *The Hidden Face of God*, (New York: Simon & Schuster, 2002) pp. xi, xiv, 138, 139.
[2]Ibid.

The Second Law of Thermodynamics

Schroeder also refers to the fact that when energy changes into matter it necessarily produces two opposing forces, matter particles and anti-matter particles which cancel each other out. But life has not been canceled out. We do have our material world. How did this happen?

Schroeder answers:

> "Life beats the odds of chaos over cosmos, but not by defeating the second law of thermodynamics. Nothing does that.
> Life wins by outwitting the second law…life has somehow gotten hold of wisdom, of information…"[3]

And British geneticist, Adam Rutherford writes:

> "Life is a process that stops your molecules from simply decaying into more stable forms. The process of living is the chemistry that perpetually holds off decay…. Our DNA encourages evolution."[4]

Evolution requires wisdom. And since the invisible wisdom contained in those first physical cells is the same invisible wisdom contained within our very own cells, we can use this understanding of how matter and anti-matter relate in addressing the issues of good and evil we face on our planet today.

Like matter and anti-matter, good and evil can be seen as two sides of the same coin. And since anti-matter cannot be defeated but can only be outwitted through wisdom, the same is true of evil—in order to defeat it, we must use wisdom.

This fact that life contains the wisdom to evolve, but anti-life does not, is the game changer! The challenge is to see evil for what it really is—a force that because it cannot evolve, can only continue to exist by finding a home in our thoughts and actions. The only way good can defeat evil is to recognize it as the anti-matter that it is and through wisdom, transcend it. This is why we are told never to fight evil with evil.

We humans can take our cue by looking to the success of evolution (interesting that the first four letters of this word spelled backwards is love). Evolution is the success of single cells outwitting anti-matter by combining into more complicated

---

[1]Ibid. p. 59.
[4]Rutherford, Adam. *Creation How Science Is Reinventing Life Itself.* (New York: Penguin Group 2013) pp. 85, 93.

and cooperative multi-cellular communities. When our own body cells cooperate with each other we thrive. Similarly, when we, as a species, cooperate with each other, we evolve. Evolution is this phenomenon on a larger planetary scale.

However, failing to realize this connectedness, when we do harm to others and to our planet we regress to a lower state, eventually ending in death.

So come along, dear reader, as we look at the results reaped from the mistaken belief that we are separate bodies and the harm we do to each other and to the earth, has no negative effect on us.

CHAPTER ONE   OUR THREATENED PLANET

"It is not adultery and fornication that is threatening humanity, but physical pollution. It is not an angry god who is threatening to destroy everything; it is a poisoned planet—poisoned by us."[5]

- Isaac Asimov and Frederik Pohl, *Our Angry Earth*

From 7200 to 1.4 Million Hiroshimas

Our present nuclear nightmare began in 1945 with the first detonation of the atomic bomb in the New Mexico desert. Then, between the years 1946 and 1958, the United States conducted 67 nuclear weapons tests in the Pacific Ocean, carrying the explosive power of 7200 Hiroshima bombs.[6] And because those radionuclides did not drift harmlessly into space, the residual radioactivity led to high rates of leukemia as well as thyroid, lung, stomach, skin and brain cancers in those Marshall Island populations.[7]

In *Arsenals of* Folly, author Richard Rhodes notes that in just the two years between 1953 and 1955, these weapons had increased from a yield of 73 megatons to 2,880 megatons.[8]

Yet, since we can never get enough of what we don't need, five years later,

---

Chapter One   Our Threatened Planet

[5] Asimov, Isaac and Pohl, Frederick. *Our Angry Earth*, (New York: Tor, 1991), p. 21.
[6] Niesse, Mark. 2009. Fallout From Nuclear Tests Leads To Health Crisis. *Associated Press*, 7 September.
[7] Ibid.
[8] Rhodes, Richard. *Arsenals of Folly: The Making Of The Nuclear Arms Race*, (New York: Alfred A. Knopf, 2007), pp. 79, 85, 87.

U.S. bombs and warheads went from 192,000 to 1.4 million Hiroshima's, making it possible to kill more than twice the dead of all the wars of the twentieth century.[9] In fact, by the 1980s, this nuclear buildup had become so successful it could pack a punch equal to ten tons of TNT for everyone in Russia, Europe, and America.[10]

And it wasn't cheap! By 1992, the Department of Defense budget in weaponry had already cost Americans taxpayers $5.5 trillion.[11]

Then as more and more nations sought nuclear weapons, the stakes became that much higher. So, in this game of catch-up, as of the mid 1980s, our planet carried 75,000 nuclear warheads[12] on its surface, all in the name of mutually-assured destruction to ensure our mutually-assured security!

The Cuban Missile Crisis

It is chilling that the fate of an entire world can sometimes hang on the decision of just one person. In his book *The Meaning of the 21st Century*, James Martin writes that during the Cuban Missile Crisis, four Soviet submarines carrying ready-to-fire nuclear weapons could have retaliated to an American ship's depth charges attack and would have, if it had not been for the wisdom of the second captain who refused to turn the key.[13]

As a result of that crisis, President Kennedy and Premier Khrushchev wisely decided that a future policy of respectful dialogue and tolerance was preferable to mutual destruction. President Kennedy realized that if we talked only with our friends and refused to talk with our enemies, we may one day have no more enemies, but just like the two sides of a coin, neither would we exist. Our very fortunate escape from a nuclear horror in that 1962 Cuban Missile Crisis may not even be possible in today's automatic nuclear-responsive world. Once those bombs start flying it will be too late for dialogue. These are weapons that are just waiting to be used in a future escalated Mideast conflict. We seem to be rushing

[9]Ibid.
[10] Rees, Martin. *Our Final Hour*, (New York: Basic Books, c2003), pp. 30,31.
[11]Ibid., p. 306.
[12]Martin, James. *The Meaning of the 21st Century*, (New York: Riverhead Books, 2006), p. 384.
[13]Ibid., pp. 120,122, 379.

toward that abyss. No wonder religious fundamentalists expect an eventual Armageddon. In his book, *Cosmos,* Carl Sagan warned that in a full nuclear exchange, the equivalent of a million Hiroshima bombs would be dropped all over the world...enough to kill a hundred billion people.[14]

Truly, there is no benefit to a nuclear game of chicken that sanity recognizes must never be played out. But there is a cost—optimal fear, over-the top trillion-dollar defense budgets, destruction of environments, and increasing distrust among nations.

Nuclear Accidents

More than 150 countries (almost 80% of the United Nation's members) warn us of the impact of nuclear detonation—either by design or by accident.[15] And nuclear accidents do happen.

In 1964 a B-52 bomber flying over North Carolina broke apart in the sky. As a result, one of its hydrogen bombs was released. The only reason it didn't detonate on United States soil was because of the failure of one of its arming stage switches.[16] In 2010, due to computer malfunction, fifty U.S. nuclear missiles suddenly went offline for an hour making them unable to communicate with launch control centers—communication that is vital in the case of a false alarm.[17]

Consider the Russian 1986 Chernobyl nuclear power reactor explosion. That accident resulted in the death of 7,000 people and eleven million were affected by cancers, birth defects, and ruined crops.[18] Furthermore, thanks to Soviet government cover-ups, none of their thirteen prior power-reactor accidents were ever reported.[19]

---

[14]Sagan, Carl. *Cosmos,* (New York: Random House, c1980), p. 322.
[15]2014.*Free Speech TV. Democracy Now-The War and Peace Report.*
24 October. Available at democracynow.org
[16]Ibid. Discussion with Eric Schlosser, author of *Illusion of Safety*
[17]Ibid.
[18]Martin, James. *The Meaning of the 21st Century,* (New York: Riverhead Books, 2006), pp. 120-122..
[19]Rhodes, Richard. *Arsenals of Folly: The Making Of The Nuclear Arms Race,* (New York: Alfred A. Knopf, 2007), p. 7.

Yet, according to Alice Slater, New York director of the Nuclear Age Peace Foundation, instead of attending the first two conferences on the impact of Nuclear Weapons, the United States plans to spend 1 trillion over the next 30 years for new bomb factories, delivery systems, missiles, submarines, airplanes and new nuclear weapons.[20]

In 2014, she noted that 26 subcritical tests involving blowing up plutonium a thousand feet below the desert floor had been done at the Nevada test site. "And now we have missiles in Poland, Romania, …Turkey. …we took missiles out of Turkey in order to get the Soviets out of Cuba, and now we've got them back in there…"[21]

Neither is nuclear energy the solution to our energy problem. According to Arnie Gundersen, former nuclear industry senior vice president, it is the least effective, most dangerous, and most expensive way to replace fossil fuel or address global warming.[22]

Scientists give three reasons for this view: cost, waste storage, and safety. First, it is not economical. We are talking billions of dollars—most of it subsidized by our tax dollars. Corporations will not take the risk, but they will take the profits. Gunderson, who has coordinated projects at 70 nuclear power plants around the country, notes that the cost of nuclear plants as of 2012 was in the 20 billion dollar range.[23]

What About Those Old Reactors?

As of 2015, 99 nuclear reactors operate at 61 nuclear power plants in the United States, many of which have reached their age of maturity.[24] When a reactor becomes too old and leaky to continue operating, the cost to decommission it is

---

[20]Slater, Alice. 2014. Discussion with Alice Slater. *Free Speech TV, "Democracy Now-The War and Peace Report"*. 4, December.
[21]Ibid.
[22]Gundersen, Arnie. 2012. Discussion with Arnie Gundersen. *Free Speech TV, "Democracy Now-The War and Peace Report"*. 12 March. Available @ democracynow.org
[23]Gundersen, Arnie. 2012. Discussion with Arnie Gundersen. *Free Speech TV, "Democracy Now-The War and Peace Report"*. 12 March. Available @ democracynow.org
[24] See: http://www.eia.gov/tools/faqs/faq.cfm?id=207&t=3
Also: 1998. Friends of the Earth Scotland. Nuclear power is no solution to climate change: *exposing the myths*. January. Available @ nirs.org

so high (in the billions of dollars) it remains undone. Profit-driven nuclear companies simply do not want to incur the high costs needed to remove those hazardous nuclear wastes. Neither do these companies always disclose vital public information about the dangers.

For example, the forty-year-old Vermont Yankee plant, owned by Entergy Corporation, had several leaks of radioactive tritium dating back to 2005. Yet, it lied about the extent of contamination to the local water supply and claimed it did not have underground pipes that could carry tritium. But it did have those underground pipes and they did leak![25]

Second, there is always the long-term dangerous problem of waste storage. How will these huge nuclear arsenals be disposed of? There really is no good place to dump nuclear waste. Asimov and Pohl warn that these dangerous radioactive materials hang on for tens of thousands of years.[26] Not just our lands, but the bottom of our oceans harbor this hazardous material.

Third, it doesn't stop at wastes. In a 60 Minutes interview in 2004,[27] Richard LaVernier noted that in putting the Los Alamos Lab in New Mexico to a security test, it was found to have had 45 major nuclear safety violations. Mock terrorists were able to penetrate it fifty percent of the time.

Another example of lax security is Trident, the UK's nuclear weapons system in Scotland. According to whistle blower William McNeilly, a submariner for the UK Trident Fleet, it is harder to get through airport security than it is to get onto a Trident nuclear weapons submarine.[28]

In 2012 three peace activists (one an 82-year-old pacifist nun) were able to infiltrate the highly enriched uranium nuclear facility in Oak Ridge, Tennessee.

---

[25]2010. In Historic Vote, Vermont Poised to Shut Down Lone Nuclear Reactor. *Free Speech TV, Democracy Now, "The War and Peace Report."* 24 February. Available on democracynow.org
[26]Asimov, Isaac and Pohl, Frederick. *Our Angry Earth*, (New York: Tor, 1991), p.79.
[27]LaVernier, Richard. 2004. Interview. *CBS 60 Minutes*. 29 August. cbsnews.com/news/nuclear-insecurity-27-08-2004/
[28]2015. *Free Speech TV. Democracy Now-The War and Peace Report.* "British Nuclear Sub Whistleblower William McNeilly Revealed Major Security Lapses". 27 May. Available at: democracynow.org/shows/2015/5/27

When asked why they did it, Sister Megan Rice explained that it wasn't to expose the lack of security so much as it was

> "...just to speak the truth about weapons of mass destruction, that everybody knows, that they're illegal, immoral."[29]

Silent Killers

Biological and chemical weapons like Sarin and VX are extremely effective agents of death. Once unleashed, they spread rapidly throughout populations. All of the big powers have these in their arsenals.

In his book *War of Nerves,* Jonathan Tucker writes about how chemical weapons were first used by the Germans in World War I, and by the end of that Great War, chemically poisoned weapons had already inflicted "one million casualties".[30]

And just as with nuclear weapons, after World War II, chemical and biological weapons research was taken up by one country after another, so that by before the end of the Cold War, this research was well on its way in America, in the prior Soviet Union, and in other countries as well.

As has already been noted, since nothing in the world happens in isolation, in the digital world, obtaining instructions to make lethal weapons is cheap and easy. Martin Rees notes that In Wasco County, Oregon, the Rajneeshee cult used Salmonella on 750 victims, and in Japan in the early 1990s, the Aum Shinrikyo sect used the nerve gas Sarin in Tokyo's subway system, harming over 3,000 people of which 12 were fatal.[31]

But just like disposal of nuclear wastes, disposal of these lethal pathogens is also a major problem. When containers begin to leak or when a newer and better pathogen gets discovered, the problem comes up of how best to get rid of the older stock. So our land and seas become the ultimate dumping ground.

---

[29] 2015. *Free Speech TV. Democracy Now-The War and Peace Report.* "How an 85-Year-Old Nun, Activists, Infiltrated Top U.S. Nuclear Site, Exposing Dangers and Urging Peace." 19, May. Available at democracynow.org
[30]Tucker, Jonathan B. *War of Nerves: Chemical Warfare From World War I to Al-Qaeda.* (New York: Pantheon Books, c2006), pp. 3.
[31]Rees, Martin. *Our Final Hour,* (New York: Basic Books, c2003), p. 49.

Thousands of cluster bombs containing mustard and Sarin have already been buried in the earth while chemical bombs and shells containing mustard gas, phosgene, and the nerve-agents Sarin and Tabun, have been dumped into our oceans. In *War of Nerves,* Jonathan Tucker writes:

> "During Operation CHASE, bulk containers of mustard agent and steel-and-concrete 'coffins' containing defective Sarin-filled M55 rockets were loaded onto a rusting Liberty ship in preparation for disposal at sea. The ship was then towed off the East Coast and scuttled in deep water."[32]

Those toxins may be sunk and buried, but like nuclear wastes, they haven't really gone away. Just because something is hidden from view doesn't mean it is neutralized.

Here again, sanity demands answers to some very important questions. What are the fruits of chemical and biological weapons? Has any good come from them? How many innocent humans have been their victims? How have they damaged our planet? Finally, who has gained great wealth by their production?

Water

Fresh water comprises only 2.5 percent of all the water on earth.[33] Like air, water is not a luxury; we all need it to survive. Along with drinking, we use water for many other reasons. This fact hits home to most of us when for some reason our water gets temporarily shut off, when our wells become polluted, or when our aquifers, rivers and lakes dry up.

World-renowned biologist, E. O. Wilson, predicts that by 2025, 40 percent of the world's population could experience water scarcity.[34] The state of California now faces an unprecedented crisis as its ground water has been depleting since the early 1900's.

---

[32]Tucker, Jonathan B. *War of Nerves: Chemical Warfare From World War I to Al-Qaeda.* (New York: Pantheon Books, c2006), pp. 217, 219.
[33] http://en.wikipedia.org/wiki/Water_distribution_on_Earth
[34]Wilson, E. O. *The Creation: An Appeal To Save Life On Earth,* (New York: 2006), p. 77.

Our aquifers, which are sources of underground fossil water, are drying up at the rate of 160 billion tons of water every year.[35] And these aquifers didn't get filled overnight; that process took thousands of years. Even back in 1991, Asimov and Pohl warned that water from these aquifers was being drawn faster than it could be replenished.[36]

And now our ground water is taking a hit. Water that can be ignited by the strike of a match is not water fit to drink! Neither is it fit for bathing or agriculture. In a new process used to recover natural gas called hydraulic fracturing or "fracking", deadly cancer-causing compounds are introduced into the earth which eventually reach and contaminate our ground water.[37]

Another disturbing aspect of fracking is the fact that this process causes methane to leak into the atmosphere. According to Climate Central, on a pound-for-pound basis, methane is a greenhouse gas that is 102 times as potent as carbon dioxide when first released.[38] But ordinary homeowners are no match for the natural gas industry's ten-year lobbying relationship with the U.S. government. As of 2011 this industry had spent $747 million[39] to prevent government from regulating their hydraulic fracking.

Asimov and Pohl have described New Orleans drinking water:

> "New Orleans draws on the Mississippi River for municipal drinking water. At the same time, the 130 oil refineries and chemical plants that line those banks use the same river to dispose of their waste products, which include such toxic chemicals as vinyl chloride and benzene…that part of Louisiana has one of the highest rates of deaths from cancer of lung, stomach and gall bladder in the country…their risk of rectal cancer doubles."[40]

However, pollution doesn't exist only in our rivers. Lakes and streams have also been compromised. Nearly half a million people in Toledo, Ohio and southeastern

---

[35]Martin, James. *The Meaning of the 21st Century*, (New York: Riverhead Books, 2006), pp. 66-67.
[36]Asimov and Pohl. *Our Angry Earth*, (New York: Tor, 1991), p. 114.
[37]nytimes.com/2015/05/05/science/earth/fracking-chemicals-detected-in-pennsylvania-drinking-water.html?_r=0
[38]*"Limiting Methane Leaks Critical to Gas, Climate Benefits"* [May 22. 2013]. Available @ climatecentral.org.
[39]*Fracking For Support: Natural Gas Industry Pumps Cash Into Congress.* [November 10. 2011] Available from Press Center @ commoncause.org
[40]Asimov, Isaac and Pohl, Frederick. *Our Angry Earth*. (New York: 1991), p. 117.

Michigan have recently had their drinking water polluted due to deadly toxins from algae blooms formed by fertilizers and raw sewage pouring into Lake Erie.

Also, the Great Lakes, numbered among the largest bodies of fresh water in the world, and a major transportation facility for shipping, have accumulated serious levels of PCB pollution.[41]

And what are PCBs? Originally used as electrical insulators, man-made polychlorinated byphenyls (PCBs) are synthetic chemicals that have been incorporated into everything from paints and pesticides to copy paper.

Since 1929, they have been introduced into every part of our globe, accumulating in the fatty tissue of lower to higher chains of life forms. Once absorbed, they accumulate in the fatty tissue of fish and animals living in water and on land, and finally in humans. Studies have shown that there is a link between PCB exposure and cancer of the digestive and lymphatic systems in humans.[42]

Again, what is hidden underwater may lend itself to convenience and profit for a few, but it eventually lends itself to damage and expense for the public at large. Asimov and Pohl described this water crisis in 1991. Yet, since then how much attention has it gotten from our elected officials or the media? Major culprits in this information vacuum have been chemical, oil, and manufacturing lobbyists.

Rivers Threatened By Toxic Sludge

In America, coal mining has left huge gaping holes on mountain tops, as well as thick, dirty, and toxic, sludge buildup contained in earthen dams. When these toxic sludge dams collapse—and they do—their poisons wreak havoc on the lives of local residents by compromising their soils and rivers.

This happened in 2008 when the Kingston Fossil Plant holding wall collapsed releasing over a billion gallons of sludge onto more than 300 acres in Harriman, Tennessee.[43]

And what was in that sludge?

---

[41]Ibid.
[42]See: What are PCBs? Available at http://www.greenfacts.org/en/pcbs/index.htm#1
[43]*O'Carroll, Eoin. 2008.* What exactly is the toxic sludge that spilled in Tennessee?*The Christian Science Monitor.* 31 December.

The sludge was a mixture of water and fly ash (fine, hollow, glassy particles of silica). Fly ash delivers more radiation into the environment than shielded nuclear waste.[44] The fly ash included trace concentrations of arsenic, lead, barium and chromium—all of which are toxic—as well as the radioactive elements uranium and thorium.

Yet, the coal industry succeeded in opposing any regulation and continued to send fly ash into its other two remaining containment ponds. Besides lining the Emory and Clinch riverbanks with dead fish, elevated arsenic levels were found in the waters adjacent to the spill. According to the inventory disclosed to the *New York Times* by the Tennessee Valley Authority, the coal plant's byproducts in just one year included "45,000 pounds of arsenic, 49,000 pounds of lead, 1.4 million pounds of barium, 91,000 pounds of chromium, and 140,000 pounds of manganese."[45] Furthermore, the T.V.A. Kingston Fossil Plant held not just one year but "many decades' worth"[46] of these deposits in its holding pond.

Eventually, when these mining sites are abandoned, who finally has to clean it up? You would think it would be the responsibility of the mining company to clean up its own mess, but as James Martin notes, it ends up costing U.S. taxpayers anywhere from $33 billion to $72 billion.[47]

For example, Duke energy, which is the biggest utility in the country, has dumped one hundred million tons of coal ash into unlined pits located next to waterways in North Carolina.[48]

In their recent spill into the Dan River in February, 2014, the company was sued by The Southern Environmental Law Center. But rather than remove that toxic waste themselves, which would cut into their profits, Duke closed their plants and just left the coal ash there for someone else to worry about. Meanwhile, that toxic waste continues to pollute nearby waterways.

---

[44]Ibid.
[45]DeWine, Shaila, 2008. At Plant in Coal Ash Spill, Toxic Deposits by the Ton. *The New York Times.* 29 December.
[46]Ibid.
[47]Martin, James. *The Meaning of the 21st Century,* (New York: Riverhead Books, 2006), p. 46.
[48]2014. The Spill at Dan River. *CBS 60 Minutes.* 7 December.

Bottled Water

Over 1,500 water bottles are consumed in the U.S. every second.[49] And because only 1 out of every 5 bottles can actually be recycled, America's landfills hold two million tons of discarded water bottles.[50]

Despite the fact that there are water treatment systems in place, the privatized bottled water industry draws from spring waters and public water systems, pouring it into plastic bottles, marketing it as being superior to our tap water, and then selling it to us at a price costing many times more.

According to the EPA, about 55 percent of our bottled water is spring water. The other 45 percent comes from the municipal water supply. And the problem with discarded plastic bottles is that it takes at least 500 years for plastic to decompose,[51] making plastic pollution a world-wide fact. Americans alone throw away 35 billion plastic water bottles every year.[52]

Compounding the problem, much of this water is being drawn from drought zone areas.[53] In spite of the fact that California is now deeply in a drought crisis, bottled water companies continue to pump fresh water from that state's public water supplies. For example, Nestle Waters North America's permit expired in 1988.[54]

Yet, because there are no state agencies tracking the amounts of this drain of public water resources by private companies, Nestle continues to profit by packaging and selling California's dwindling water supply as Arrowhead 100 percent Mountain Spring Water.

Tens of millions of gallons of water have been drawn from pristine streams of the San Bernardino National Forest by Nestle.[55]

---

[49]onegreenplanet.org/animalsandnature/whats-the-problem-with-plastic-bottles/
[50]See: thewaterproject.org/bottled_water_wasteful
[51]Back2tap.com
[52] http://ecowatch.com/2014/04/07/22-facts-plastic-pollution-10-things-can-do-about-it/
[53]Lurie, Julia. 2014. Does Your Bottled Water Come From A Drought Zone? *Atlantic.* Dnews. 15 August.
[54]Picchi, Aimee, 2015. Should bottled water companies sell national forest water?*CBS Moneywatch.* 20 March. See investigation by James Ion published in The Desert Sun Newspaper, March 8, 2015. Available at onegreenplanet.org.
[55]Ibid.

And Wal-Mart also continues to bottle water from California's Sacramento Municipal Water supply at a cost of 99 cents for every 748 gallons, and then sells it for 88 cents per gallon. So for every $1 of water Wal-Mart buys of California's dwindling water supply, they make $658.24.[56] Meanwhile, Californians struggle with an ever decreasing water supply.

The World's Water

Neither have the rest of the world's water systems escaped crisis. With little or no treatment systems in place, many of Eastern Europe's rivers have been polluted by open sewage.[57] Fresh water levels are also dropping in China, Russia, Egypt and Nigeria.[58]

In China, almost 2700 miles of waterways will need to be built in order to divert water from southern China to the northern dried up river areas at a cost of nearly $80 billion.[59] India too, is now in a full-fledged water crisis produced by open sewage and decay, dropping water tables, and industrial pollution. Irresponsible fish farming, sewage dumping, and the damming of fresh water rivers have all left their mark.[60]

in South America, rivers in Ecuador have been turned into cesspools. In *Confessions of an Economic Hit Man,* author John Perkins writes that during its operations between 1964 and 1990, Texaco dumped billions of gallons of toxic crude into the country's rivers. Then, in 2001, Texaco was sold to Chevron, making it even more difficult for communities to claim damages. [61] Thirty-thousand residents of Orellana and Sucumbios provinces in Ecuador were victims of these oil drilling operations. Billions of gallons of cancer causing toxic crude fouled previously pristine rivers, lakes, and soils. Sixty-one year old Ecuadorian villager, Maria Aguinda, who helped bring a landmark case against Chevron for

---

[56]2015. Courage Campaign. "Demand that Wal-Mart stop bottling water from drought-stricken CA! act.couragecampaign.org/sign/WalmartDrought_CC/
[57]Asimov, Isaac and Pohl, Frederick. *Our Angry Earth.* (New York: 1991), p. 118.
[58]Ibid.
[59]Doane, Seth. 2014. China turns to drastic measures to avoid water crisis. *CBS News.* 28 November.
[60]Asimov, Isaac and Pohl, Frederick. *Our Angry Earth.* (New York: 1991),
[61]Perkins, John. *Confessions of an Economic Hit Man,* (San Francisco, CA: Berrett-Koehler, c2004), p. xviii.

polluting her rainforest, had this to say: "Before I die they have to pay me for the dead animals, and for what they did to the river, and the water and the earth."[62]

Our Oceans

Our oceans have become the ultimate host to plastic rubbish, toxic pesticides, nerve agents, nuclear warheads, nuclear wastes, and oil spills.

Trapped in the movement of ocean currents in the Pacific Ocean are two growing islands of floating plastic waste and debris which is twice the size of Texas. It consists of two parts—a western patch near Japan and an eastern patch near Hawaii and California and it can be seen from space.[63]

A 2010 study showed China as the top offender having dumped nearly 5 billion pounds of plastic waste "everything from hard hats to fishing nets to tires to toothbrushes."[64]

According to Eco Watch,[65] annually more than 1 million plastic bags are used worldwide every minute. It takes 500 to 1000 years for plastic to degrade. Plastic chemicals alter hormones in the human body and 93 percent of Americans age six or older, test positive for BPA.

In the Los Angeles area ten metric tons of plastic fragments (plastic bags, straws, and soda bottles) are carried into the Pacific Ocean every day. And because sea creatures ingest these toxicants, liver and stomach abnormalities increase in fish and birds.

The Gulf of Mexico

During 3 months in 2010, as a result of BP's deep-sea drilling operations, a total of 4.9 million barrels of crude oil leaked into the Gulf of Mexico. [66] Those oil plumes, along with added chemical dispersants that were sprayed on the surface

---

[62]Pachico, Valeria. 2011. Indigenous Ecuadoran Woman humbles US oil giant. *Chevron/Toxico*. 22 February. Available @ chevrontoxico.com.
[63] 2014. Kamp, Karin. Plastic Junk Litters our Oceans, Killing Sea Life—And it's Getting Worse. 15, October. Available @ billmoyers.com.
[64]Ibid.
[65]http://ecowatch.com/2014/04/07/22-facts-plastic-pollution-10-things-can-do-about-it/
[66]2011. Hance, Jeremy.Gulf of Mexico bottom still coated in oil, recovery long way off. 21 February. Available @ http://news.mongabay.com/2011/0221-hance_oilspill.html

to hide the damage, threaten the ocean column and the lives of Gulf fishermen for years to come. And despite BP's denial, according to the Environmental News Network, there is still an oil layer nearly four inches thick which is steadily killing marine life on 2600 miles of the Gulf floor.[67]

A Dwindling Necessity

In *The Human, The Orchid, And The Octopus,* Jacques Cousteau wrote:

> "…scientists discovered that liquid water, which brought forth life on Earth, exists nowhere else in great quantities in the solar system…water is rare in infinity," …and …"we should prize it, preserve it, conserve it."[68]

We haven't done that.

Outer Space

It turns out that not just our planet, but the space surrounding it, also reflects our actions. Cousteau questioned the arrogance of scientists looking to produce a colorful aurora by setting off a hydrogen bomb, referred to as the Rainbow Bomb, in the Van Allen belt.[69] This is an area around the earth consisting of charged particles that effect life on our planet. He was also very concerned about the destruction caused by supersonic fighter planes of the ozone layer which protects us from radiation. He warned that science needs to be regulated along the lines of caution—not just reacting to damage already done, but preventing it in the first place!

Space is also becoming another final resting place for our junk. As of September, 2011, there were 22,000 objects in orbit as well as countless smaller ones that could do damage to human-carrying spaceships and valuable satellites.[70] Because these man-made objects orbit our planet at extremely high speeds, there is a great potential for damage should any of these orbiting objects (even as small

---

[67]Ibid.
[68]Cousteau, Jacques. *The Human, The Orchid, And The Octopus*, (New York: Bloomsbury USA, c2007), p. 202.
[69]Ibid, p. 199.
[70] 2011.The National Research Council. 2 September.

as a spec of paint) collide with some other object. It is not just the size, but the speed at which they are traveling, that makes them so dangerous.[71]

Cousteau warned that if one of these small objects could shatter a satellite it could also shatter one of the orbiting nuclear reactors which have been launched into space. One tenth of these nuclear reactors have already ruptured.[72]

Our Soils - Dead or Alive?

Food is only as good as the soil in which it grows, but as James Martin notes, ninety per-cent of complex quality topsoil is being lost 17 times faster than it is being replaced.[73] And soils compromised by pesticides and pollution do not produce nutritious food. At best, we eat fruits and vegetables with little or no vitality; at worst, we compromise our health with poisons.

According to Dr. Don Huber, Professor Emeritus of plant pathology at Purdue University, animal scientists have documented infection of an unnamed pathogen found in soy bean feed and corn feed sprayed with the GMO herbicide Round Up as well as in the soil in which these feed plants have grown.[74]

He explains that this infection has resulted in infertility and still births in cattle, pigs, chickens, and horses which have been fed with the treated feed. The pathogen is very small and can be seen only in an electron microscope. A common hitchhiker with other organisms, it is found inside fungi and grows in the presence of bacteria. It kills a fertilized egg in 24 to 48 hours.

He also notes that because Round Up is an herbicide that represses resistance to its ingredient, glyphosate (a biocide combining a metallic ion with an organic compound), it suppresses and immobilizes the organism that makes manganese as well as other necessary plant nutrients (manganese is critical in destroying toxins).

---

[71]Asimov, Isaac and Pohl, Frederick. *Our Angry Earth*, (New York: Tor,1991), pp. 155, 156, 159.
[72]Cousteau, Jacques. *The Human, The Orchid, And The Octopus*, (New York: Bloomsbury USA, c2007), p. 93.
[73]Martin, James. *The Meaning of the 21st Century*, (New York: Riverhead Books, 2006), p. 72.
[74]Huber, Dr. Don. Dr. Huber's Warning. Available @
action.fooddemocracynow.org/sign/dr_hubers_warning/.

As a result, soybean feed and corn feed have a 40% reduction in manganese and other essential nutrients.[75] Because this chelating ingredient in Roundup is so effective, it is widely used. And, since there is no void in soils, when necessary nutrients like manganese are killed off, they are replaced by fungi and other destructive microorganisms. With continued use of glyphosate, entire groups of organisms cease to exist in plants and soils. Food Democracy Now gives us some disturbing statistics:

> "In 2010 more than 365 million acres were planted worldwide with genetically engineered (GMO) seeds. The U.S. leads with more than 165 million acres of GMO crops. Monsanto owns patents of sugar beets planted in the U.S.—all genetically modified to be resistant to the weed killer Roundup.
> In 2007, more than 185,000,000 lbs. of Roundup were applied to U.S. crops, the same year that the Bush administration halted the reporting of herbicide's application rates."[76]

Dow's genetically engineered corn uses the herbicide 2,4-D which is a synthetic *auxin* (plant hormone) prone to drifting. Along with the benefit of encouraging weed resistance, 2,4-D is also dangerous to human health.[77] As the commercial use of 2,4-D expands throughout the environment, it causes damage to neighboring farmers' crops, threatening U.S. food and agriculture.

Organic farmers have discovered that genes can actually transfer from genetically engineered species to non-genetically-engineered species— Monsanto's genetically modified seeds have already contaminated their organic plants, making it illegal for organic farmers to continue to market their own produce.

In 2002 the Saskatchewan Organic Directorate (SOD) launched a class-action lawsuit against Monsanto and Aventis for damages caused by genetically engineered canola crops having spread and contaminated their organic crops.[78]

---

[75]Ibid.
[76]Huber, Dr. Don. Dr. Huber's Warning. Available @
action.fooddemocracynow.org/sign/dr_hubers_warning/.
[77]*foodandwaterwatch.org/food/genetically-engineered-foods/24-d-corn/n.wikipedia.org/wiki/Agent_Orange.*
[78]planetark.org/dailynewsstory.cfm/newsid/13999/story.htm

The Advantage of Patenting

Monsanto's genetically modified seeds do not produce seeds of their own, thus forcing farmers to buy new seeds for each new season.[79] Furthermore, thanks to Monsanto's patents, "if the farmers have any seeds left over, they must agree not to save and replant them in the future."[80] In other words, once hooked, farmers have little choice but to become permanent purchasers of Monsanto seed. Also, if seed dealers stock Monsanto seeds they are not allowed to stock competitors' seeds.[81]

Although many look to organic farming as the better alternative, organic fruits and vegetables are still too expensive for most people. We may be able to change a small part of our diet, but the major portion of our grocery shopping still consists of foods that are not properly labeled.

Our Forests

Deforestation is another culprit in soil erosion. Once the forests are gone, the soils are permanently compromised. When oil was discovered under the Amazon rain forests in Ecuador, those precious trees didn't stand a chance. Neither did the health of the local residents.

Also, nature's tool for balancing our atmosphere has always been her forests—every two-ton tree serves us by absorbing nearly seven tons of carbon dioxide in its lifetime.[82] In *The Sixth Extinction,* author Terry Glavin tells us that three-quarters of the planet's old forests have already been cut down along with their ecologies.[83] That leaves us with a lot of unabsorbed carbon dioxide.

Unfortunately, once forests are destroyed, carbon dioxide, water vapor, and methane trap even more heat, so our atmosphere literally becomes a greenhouse. Countries like China, Russia, and India, as well as countries in Eastern Europe

---

[79]Reich, Robert B. *Saving Capitalism For the Many, Not the Few.* (New York Alred A. Knopf, 2015). P. 35.
[80]Ibid., p. 34.
[81]Ibid.
[82]Asimov. Isaac and Pohl, Frederick. *Our Angry Earth,* (New York: Tor, 1991), pp. 40, 42.
[83]Glavin, Terry. *The Sixth Extinction,* (New York: Thomas Dunne Books/St. Martin's Press, 2007), P. 202.

and South America, are joining the United States in contributing to this giant heat trap.

Replacing these forests can take years—even centuries. And, cutting down tropical forest areas to grow bio-fuels such as palm-oil is not the way to address global warming. Bio-fuel heats up the atmosphere even more.[84] Neither is mining friendly to forests. In Russia, whole forests have been completely killed off by the results of mining activity.[85]

Wars and Soils

We don't often associate warfare with soil destruction, but we should. Just think of all the bombs that have exploded on our planet since the beginning of the 20th century.

The two world wars left Europe devastated. In Vietnam, the defoliant Agent Orange killed off so much of the existing plant life, its soil was no longer productive.[86] Nor did soils benefit from the Korean War, the atomic bombs dropped on Japan, and all the cluster bombs dropped on Laos soils. One can only imagine what poor condition the soil as well as plant life in the Middle East is in by now as a result of all the bombing on that part of our planet.

Our Atmosphere

Dust produced by coal-fired energy causes the deaths of nearly 24,000 people per year.[87] In this fossil-fuel dependent world of ours, the level of atmospheric carbon dioxide is compounding rapidly. In his book, *Eaarth*, Bill McKibbon notes that we are no longer living on the same planet.[88] By changing the spelling of Earth he emphasizes this fact. He reminds us that NASA scientists have determined that 350 parts per million (ppm) is the safe upper limit of carbon

---

[84] 2007. Discussion with George Monbiot, author of Heat. *Free Speech TV, "Democracy Now-The War and Peace Report".* 18 May. Available @ democracynow.org.
[85] Asimov, Isaac and Pohl, Frederick. *Our Angry Earth,* (New York: Tor, 1991), pp. 80, 81.
[86] Asimov, Isaac and Pohl, Frederick. *Our Angry Earth,* (New York: Tor, 1991), pp. 136, 137.
[87] Martin, James. *The Meaning of the 21st Century,* (New York: Riverhead Books, 2006), p. 126.
[88] McKibben, Bill. *Eaarth: making a life on a tough new planet.* (New York: St. Martin's Griffin, 2011, c2010.

dioxide in the atmosphere. Yet, according to the United Nations' World Meteorological Organization, in 2013:

> "…concentrations of carbon dioxide reached nearly 400 parts per million, the highest level in at least 800,000 years. As oceans absorb the increased carbon, ocean acidification has reached a rate that is "unprecedented at least over the last 300 million years."[89]

But carbon dioxide isn't our only problem. Methane which comes from bacteria, rotting matter, coal mining, and hydraulic fracking, is even more problematic, as it is many times more potent *than* carbon dioxide.[90] As this gas is released from melting ice in vast areas of Siberia and Canada and from the bottom of our oceans, the cycle of global warming actually begins to feed on itself.

Other gases, which are not natural but man-made synthetic gases such as CFCs (chlorofluorocarbons), are even worse than methane. To say that their effects last a very long time is an understatement.

These ozone-destroying molecules remain in our atmosphere, reducing protection from ultraviolet rays for centuries.[91] And as extreme changes in weather cause more intense thunderstorms, storm water that reaches deep into the stratosphere reacts with the CFCs that are already there, increasing the rate of ozone depletion.[92]

Heat and Ocean – A Deadly Mix

Heat is an energy that drives wind and waves. And, since everything on our planet is connected, as our atmosphere gets increasingly warmer, so do our oceans. Hurricane Katrina's recent destruction, one of the fiercest hurricanes in recorded history, covered a distance from New Orleans to Alabama.[93] And because ocean water is even more effective in absorbing heat than ice which just reflects it, the problem compounds—glaciers are melting at an alarming rate.

---

[89] 2014. *Free Speech TV, Democracy Now-"The War and Peace Report"*, 9 September. Available @ democracynow.org.
[90] 2013. Discussion with documentary film-maker Josh Fox. "Gasland Part II." *Free Speech TV, Democracy Now-The War and Peace Report.* 12 July. Available @ democracynow.org.
[91] Asimov, Isaac and Pohl, Frederick. *Our Angry Earth*, (New York: Tor, 1991), pp. 42, 95, 96.
[92] Ibid.
[93] livescience.com/22522-hurricane-katrina-facts.html.

Within just one week a part of the Arctic Ice Cap almost twice the size of the UK had melted into the ocean. And the potential for this melting of Antarctica icecaps puts southern Florida's 1,200 mile coastline in danger.

Is one more degree of warming that serious?

Scientists agree that an increase of just one degree leads to automatic positive feedback. In other words one degree will automatically go to two. James Martin warns ..."We are fooling with a system of massive forces."[94] He notes that there are three columns of warm moisture laden air that hover over Southeast Asia, Brazil, and Africa, which if pushed over a critical point, could combine into one huge current. He writes that the Gulf Stream alone carries within it the equivalent of 75 Amazon rivers.[95]

But global warming will increase no matter what we do now because the heat engine has already been set in motion. Yet, unbelievably, we continue to hear from the climate-change deniers. Wealthy oil interests interfere with scientific warnings by producing fake science reports, taking down web sites, and playing down the seriousness of this crisis. When the best advice regarding fossil fuel is "to keep it in the ground," what are the actions of Shell, Chevron, ExxonMobil, Total, and BP? These big five are laying out $1.1 trillion to unlock even more new hydrocarbon reserves from some of the most inaccessible locations on the planet.[96] But, apparently not all shareholders agree with this 9-year plan of oil extraction. Chevron activist shareholders are calling for the company to slash this upstream capital spending and return the $1.1 trillion to its shareholders instead.[97]

"Under The Dome"

This ground-breaking documentary going viral in China, is greatly influencing a growing movement in that country to replace the use of fossil fuel with renewable

---

[94]Martin, James. *The Meaning of the 21st Century,* (New York: Riverhead Books, 2006), pp. 108-110.
[95]Ibid.
[96]2015. Bowers, Simon. And Davies, Harry. "Oil company bosses' bonuses linked to $1tn spending on extracting fossil fuels" *The Guardian..* 25 May.
[97]Ibid.

energy.[98]   It describes how the dangerous haze of air pollution contains 2.5 micrometers in carcinogens and heavy metals. Children only two months old that have never been outside already have pneumonia. Many young children have never seen a blue sky, clouds, or stars at night and there have been 500,000 premature deaths due to air pollution and lung cancer, an increase by 465%.[99]

The Best Things in Life are Not Free

Who would argue the importance of clean air? Like our need for water, we all must breathe. But noxious fumes that are daily emitted into our large cities have caused breathing difficulty for millions of people. In America health costs due to asthma each year are now in the billions of dollars.[100] Pediatric emergency rooms and school absences attest to that fact. But how realistic is it to expect powerful industries to voluntarily stop their polluting when their decisions are always based solely on profit? What good is a planet that has no healthy place for our children and grandchildren to live and breathe?

One thing is for sure; this planet can, and will, turn on us to correct itself. Will we demand that our elected leaders face up to the fact that nature plays by her own rules?

Sooner rather than later, is definitely advisable.

---

[98]"Papish, Jonathan. 2015. Under The Dome" Documentary on China's Pollution by Chai Jing. Available at: youtube.com/watch?v=Zvj8ITg7P7o
[99]Ibid.
[100]Moyers, Bill. *Moyers on America A Journalist And His Times.* (New York: New Press: Distributed by W.W. Norton, c2004), p.71.

CHAPTER TWO   MEDIA

"Parent corporations, advertisers, and commercial interests operate invisible levers over the news a great deal of the time. The largest thing that we are not reporting is the simply grotesque inequity between societies,...these huge growing problems in the world that nobody is addressing."[101]

-Tom Fenton, *Bad News*

When asked about the inconsistent results of his Warren Commission report on the assassination of President Kennedy, Allen Dulles wasn't too worried. His view was that Americans don't read these reports.[102]

That may have been partly true then, but today's internet with its social networking has changed the playing field. It is now possible to have access to instant communication with anyone in the world, and this has resulted in a global awareness from which governments and corporations cannot hide. As this super-organism of mind grows, its demand for freedom and transparency multiplies—reflecting for us how true it is that the whole is greater than the sum of its parts.

Looking back, most of us can remember where we were on 9/11. We watched in shock and disbelief as those events unfolded on our television screens. But few of us had any concept of the events that brought it about.

We had seen plenty of tabloid television but very little comprehensive foreign news coverage. Our minds were like sponges ready to soak up whatever

---

Chapter Two   Media

[101]Fenton, Tom. *Bad News: The Decline of Reporting, The Business of News, And The Danger To Us All,* (New York: Regan Books, c2005), pp. 18, 26.
[102]Ruppert C., Michael. *Crossing the Rubicon,* (Gabriola island, B.C.: New Society Publishers, c2004), P. 54.

information was fed to us by our commercial media. And soak it up we did. But there was much of which we were ignorant. News reports on speeches of public support for the Iraq war were focused on Cheney and Rumsfeld, while reports on speeches in opposition to the war, including Edward Kennedy and Robert Byrd were relegated to back pages."[103]

How much was media reporting on how the Saudi royal family since the early 1980s, in order to keep peace with its Wahhabi clerics, had been footing the bill to spread a radical extremist religious doctrine all around the world?[104] Not too many of us were even familiar with the word Wahhabi. It was not in our nightly newscasts that thousands of these schools had been established.

Many of us may have ignorantly assumed that Middle-East tension was confined to Israel and Palestine. Because of our naiveté, it was possible to be given a picture of this tragic day in terms that we had very little ability to properly discern.

But why were we not more informed? Furthermore, how many of us on September 11 were familiar with the name Osama bin Laden? He may not have been familiar to many Americans but he certainly was extremely popular in the hills of Afghanistan. Children there even had bin Laden's face on sugar candy ball wrappings with his finger pointed to the tip of a rocket."[105]

Suddenly our media began showing us photos of a bearded bin Laden wearing flowing robes and speaking to us from caves in the mountains of Afghanistan. His appearance absolutely decried modern capitalism. However, his image was a far cry from that of his family, which owned and ran the largest global construction business in the Islamic world.[106] His Saudi family also enjoyed social connections

---

[103]Schlesinger, Jr. Arthur M. War And The American Presidency. (New York, 2004), p. 33.
[104]Gold, Dore. *Hatred's Kingdom: How Saudi Arabia Supports The New Global Terrorism*, (Washington, DC: Regnery Pub.: Lanham, MD, Distributed by National Book Network, c2003), p. 126.

[105]Scheuer, Michael. *Imperial Hubris: why the West is losing the war on terror.* (Washington, D.C.:B rassey's. c2004), p. 105. From New York Times article written by Daniel Berger.

[106]Ruppert, Michael C. *Crossing The Rubicon.* (Gabriola Island, B.C.: New Society Publishers, c2004), p. 127.

---

with top levels in our American government.[107] Saddam Hussein was another unfamiliar name to many of us. Yet, our country had been cooperating with him long before 9/11. It certainly was in our national interest to be better informed about these things. We are now.

The 2008 Economic Crisis

Commercial media also failed to keep us informed of the moves that led up to the recent global economic crisis. Before it hit, where were the debates on the wisdom of repealing the Glass-Steagall Act?

Repealing this act allowed big commercial banks to merge with investment banks, permitting them to speculate with their depositor's money. Hedge fund speculators were now able to cover themselves with insurance protection while they turned huge and quick profits repackaging a fraudulent market scheme of sub-prime mortgages into pools of dangerous securities

They sold these securities to pension funds and insurance firms. But when it became apparent that there was no true value to these securities, the entire global economic system became threatened. So Wall Street tossed their hot potato into the hands of taxpayers worldwide. This bailout with taxpayer money (to the tune of trillions of dollars) was the result of allowing commercial banks to merge with investment banks, which is what the Glass-Steagall Act forbade.[108]

And where was the wisdom in The Commodity Futures Modernization Act written in 2000 by Republican Senator Phil Gramm calling for de-regulation of commodity futures and swaps?[109]

These actions were not on front page news but they should have been. Yet some were sounding an alarm. Brooksley Born, chair of the Commodities Futures Trading Commission (CFTC), spoke out against doing away with regulation. But

[107]Ibid.
[108]Ibid.2010. The true cost of the bank bailout. Needtoknow on PBS. 3 September. ww.pbs.org/wnet/need-to-know/economy/the-true-cost-of-the-bank-bailout/3309/
[109]Corn, David. 2008. "Foreclosure Phil". A summary of the events leading up to the foreclosure crisis. *Mother Jones.* July and August.

she was ignored by the media and soon quieted by Larry Summers and Alan Greenspan, the economic wizards of the day.[110]

Had there been more objective news coverage of her warning, we might have been spared our 2008 economic crisis in which 23 million jobs were lost, 93 million lost their health insurance and 1 million lost their homes.[111]

It seems it was our turn to taste the same bitter economic disaster capitalism that has been the experience of our third-world neighbors. Was there any reason to think that greed and power-grabbing would not appear within our own borders?

When media is controlled by private for-profit conglomerates, what do you think will take priority? Will it be expensive domestic and foreign journalism that keeps citizens informed and governments honest? Or will it be inexpensive entertainment, endless commercials, and low-cost reality shows that keep citizens distracted?

Another media failure was on the use of depleted uranium in the Gulf War which caused horrible disfigurements in the faces and bodies of Iraqi children born in those locations.[112] Hospital records showing photographs of these children never appeared on our television screens, but Arabs saw them.

In the run-up to the Iraq war, government officials who pushed for war were actually assisted by the media. Much praise and comment was heaped upon our high-tech, precision-guided weaponry, as if Iraqi citizens had nothing to fear.

However, in *The Shock Doctrine,* author Naomi Klein includes what Yasime Musa, a Baghdad mother of three, said during the bombings: "Not a single minute passes by without hearing and feeling a drop of a bomb somewhere. I don't think that a single meter in the whole of Iraq is safe."[113] Unfortunately, any journalist who took a different view to the Iraq war put his or her career at risk. Media

---

[110]2009. The Warning. *PBS Frontline.* 20 October.
[111]2015. Wall Street's Threat to the American Middle Class. Robert Reich blog. 30 January.
[112]Chopra, Deepak. *Peace is the Way: Bringing War and Violence to an End,* (New York: Harmony Books, c2005), pp. 79, 80.
[113]Klein, Naomi. *The Shock Doctrine: The Rise of Disaster Capitalism,* (New York: Metropolitan Books/Henry Holt, 2007), p. 332.

personalities such as Phil Donahue and Peter Arnett, who did challenge that war propaganda, were soon silenced.[114]

Journalist Chris Hedges, after fifteen years working for the *New York Times,* was made to leave because of his "public denouncing" of the Iraq War.[115]

Or how much TV coverage followed up on the millions of Iraqis who, as a result of our invasion had to flee their homes with no passport, no job, no money, and no shelter? Two-and-a-half million Iraqis fled to Jordan, Lebanon, Egypt, Turkey, the Gulf States and, most of all, Syria, which hosted one-and-a-half million[116] (all of which has surely contributed to the ISIS conflict).

And since these Iraqis no longer lived in Iraq, they could not exercise their votes in their country's elections—so much for our goal to bring democracy to their country. At the very least, the plight of these refugees deserved much more coverage than was given them.

Here in our own country how much reporting was done on the case of nine-year old Kevin, a Canadian citizen who, with his Iranian parents, was kept at a detention center in Texas for six weeks? [117]

After his parents had been tortured in Iran and were finally able to escape on a flight to Canada, they were forced off the plane in Puerto Rico and detained in Texas. This action by our government was not on our nightly news but it certainly was in Canada; it was headline news every day! After continued protests by outraged Canadians, the family's attorney, Andrew Brouwer was able to get a permit for the family to return to Canada on a temporary basis. Meanwhile, how many Americans were aware that 200 more children like Kevin have been held in detention in Texas?[118]

---

[114]2007. *Free Speech TV, "Democracy Now, The War and Peace Report"*, Discussion with Norman Solomon on his book, *War Made Easy.* 29 May Available @ democracynow.org.

[115]Hedges, Chris. 2012. Bill Moyers interview with Chris Hedges. "Capitalism's Sacrifice Zones". 20 July. Available @ billmoyers.com.

[116]2008. "Exodus: "Where Will Iraq Go Next?" Free Speech TV, *"Democracy Now, The War And Peace Report",* 31 March. Available @ democracynow.org.

[117] 2007. 9-Year Old Canadian Citizen and Iranian Parents Arrive in Toronto After Six Weeks in Texas Immigration Jail. Free Speech TV, *"Democracy Now, The War and Peace Report"* 22 March. Available @ democracynow.org.

[118]Ibid.

When did the term "water-boarding" first come into the American consciousness? How is it that the shameful events at Abu Ghraib and Guantanamo went on for so long before we even became aware of it? Americans didn't know about this torture, but Arabs did.

Nor has there been much media follow-up on the human trauma of ICE's rounding up of illegal immigrants. Separating parents from their young children. and holding them in far away detention centers certainly would seem to deserve at least a little bit of follow-up.

Never did we read in our history books that our ethnic ancestors applied for legal permission to enter the New World. We might question, instead, what is so wrong in Mexico that is causing all these families to escape?

In a Bill Moyers interview with Chris Hedges, Hedges pointed out that The North Atlantic Free Trade Agreement (NAFTA), which destroyed Mexican subsistence farming by replacing it with its corporate agriculture, had a lot to do with it. It is estimated NAFTA drove three million Mexican farmers into bankruptcy.[119]

While America's public institutions, Medicare, Social Security, and social programs are under attack by those who see these "entitlements" as the cause of our Federal Deficit, how much media coverage has focused on the trillions of dollars spent on the wars in Iraq and Afghanistan? Or the billions of dollars handed out to corporations each year in the form of government contracts, deregulation, public land grabs, and tax relief giveaways?

Where is the media exposure on "sweet deals" for wealthy investors as they extract billions of our tax dollars in the form of "subsidies" from cities all across our country?[120]

Instead of using their own money (which they have plenty of) to finance their sports stadiums, business parks, retail mega-stores, oil drilling and agriculture,

---

[119]2012. BillMoyers interview with Chris Hedges. "Capitalism's Sacrifice Zones". 20 July. Available @ billmoyers.com.
[120]Johnston, David Cay. *Free Lunch: How The Wealthiest Americans Enrich Themselves At Government Expense* (London: Penguin Books Ltd., 2008).

they coerce city, state, and federal governments into subsidizing them with taxes paid by working Americans.[121]

Fake News You Can Trust

Filtering of news is only one step away from actual distortion of news in which public relations experts hire front groups who disguise themselves as reporters or scientific and medical professionals in order to promote their corporate agendas. For example, Video News Reports (VNRs) are often disguised as public messages. These PR strategies, referred to as "payola pundit" scandals,[122] were utilized by the Bush administration to advance such causes as the push for the Iraq war, the No Child Left Behind program, denial of global warming, and the reforming of Medicare.

One of those VNRs, produced for TCS Daily Science Roundtable, (the word Science gave it a certain respectability) denied that global warming caused hurricanes, blaming hurricanes on the cycles of nature itself. It was aired on television and backed by Exxon Mobile's Lobbying Firm. As of November, 2006, forty-six stations in twenty-two states were operating this way, in violation of FCC rules.[123] This distortion of news was illegal, yet it was successfully employed to discredit global warming.

But what the news media was not reporting were the warnings of Dr. James Hansen who for twenty-five years headed NASA's Goddard Institute of Space Studies and climate research center. Starting in 1988 he began to warn the United States government about global warming and climate change. But Americans never got this information because his warnings were censored. Finally, in 2006 he went public about the direct attempts of the government to silence him.[124] Dr. Hansen has identified 350 parts per million CO2 as the safe upper limit for carbon

---

[121]Ibid.

[122]Conason, Joe. *It Can Happen Here: Authoritarian Peril In The Age Of Bush,* (New York: Thomas Dunne Books/St. Martin's Press. 2007) P. 121.

[123]2006. Free Speech TV, *"Democracy Now-The War and Peace Report"*, Discussion with Diane Farsetta of Center for Media and Democracy, co-author of study investigating VNRs. "Still Not the News". 14 November. Available @ democracynow.org.

[124]2008. Free Speech TV, *"Democracy Now-The War and Peace Report"*, Discussion with Dr. James Hansen. 21 March. Available @ democracynow.org

in the atmosphere and he has worked tirelessly to warn of the dangers of the Keystone XL pipeline.

Who Controls Media?

Since the 1990s this concentration of media ownership by mega corporations has steadily increased. In February, 2009, as the switch was made from analog TV to digital broadcasting, the giveaway of our public airwaves to private ownership resulted in each of the more than 1700 private broadcasting companies getting their channels tripled and quadrupled.[125]

A survey by the Alliance for Community Media showed that Comcast, AT&T, and Verizon, all applied for state funding through this new state franchising law.[126] In spite of the fact that the airwaves are public property under U.S. law, and broadcasters receive their licenses from the FCC only on the condition that they serve the public interest, it remains to be seen how many of these thousands of new channels are likely to be available for independent public access, educational and children's programming, women and minority issues, and local government access.

Net Neutrality

The First Amendment of the Constitution protects free speech from intervention by government power. But what about intervention by private power which as we have seen, exercises greater influence on our government than do its ordinary citizens? Net neutrality is the next great challenge for Americans as cable providers vie for greater control over the internet. The Internet Freedom Preservation Act of 2008 (HR5353)[127] legislates that high-speed internet services be kept open, available, and affordable to all Americans. Yet a May, 2008 survey by the Alliance for Community Media (ACM) found that Public, Educational and

---

[125] Why did we switch from analog to digital signal?Answers.yahoo.com
[126]Alliance For Community Media, Assessing the Damage: Survey shows that state video franchise laws bring no rate relief while harming public benefits.
[127]SavetheInternet.com.

Government (PEG) services had already seen a decrease in their funding and availability.[128]

Then on January 14, 2014 the U.S. Court of Appeals struck down the FCC's "no blocking" and nondiscrimination rules of the 2010 open internet order.[129] This action would allow big companies to dictate which sites load quickly, slowly, or not at all? High-speed wireless internet service could become accessible only to those wealthy enough to pay for it, putting most Americans on an unequal footing.

Fortunately, in February of 2015 the FCC Chairman Tom Wheeler, upheld net neutrality by backing the regulation of Internet service as a public utility.[130] By referring to the Title II protections, he states that the internet is not like one-way media (television, radio, or newspapers), but instead is two-way media and since it is two-way communications the public must be protected from discrimination by the carrier.

Four million responses on the FCC website had succeeded in a demand for net neutrality. Grassroots Activism like Free Press, Demand Progress, Fight for the Future, and Color of Change worked tirelessly to achieve this Title II protection.[131]

Cozy Relationships with Governments

A pact between a government and a corporate-controlled media means much chicanery that occurs in the world can be withheld from its citizens. The latest exposure of NSA total surveillance on Americans is a good example. Governments can also demand that high-tech companies filter out undesirable information from internet searches or can take down entire sites. For example, in China when Beijing University students were asked to identify photos taken of

---

[128]Alliance For community Media. Survey shows that state video franchise laws bring no rate relief while harming public benefits. May 2008 online survey.
[129]2015. Free Speech TV, *"Democracy Now-The War and Peace Report"*, FCC's Net Neutrality Shift a Victory for Open Internet & Grassroots Activism Against Cable Giants.. 21 March. Available @ democracynow.org
[130]Ibid.
[131]Ibid.

the tanks in the 1989 Tieneman Square Massacre, amazingly not one had any knowledge of that event—no one could explain it.[132]

Now, one could argue that it wasn't ignorance but fear that motivated these students. But does that really matter? Whether the underlying cause was fear which resulted in panapticon-like behavior or just the result of ignorance, the fact remains that whenever information and/or free speech is suppressed, human rights and freedoms are forfeited.

This happens across our world as media domination is being concentrated in fewer and fewer hands and as oligarchs attempt to control what we hear and see.[133] Bill Moyers has commented on how in Italy, one man, Silvio Berlusconi, has owned 90 percent of the media, his control extending across TV networks, public airwaves, publishing houses, newspapers and magazines, as well as movie production and distribution.[134] Nevertheless, during Italy's recent economic crisis, the world has watched Silvio Berlusconi's fall from grace.

In Britain, as a result of illegal phone hacking by News Corp. journalists, Rupert Murdoch's media empire was publicly exposed and discredited as he and his son James Murdoch were called to testify before the British Parliament. Murdoch's 2007 acquisition of the Wall St. Journal for $5 billion[135] was another step closer to media concentration.

And when it comes to profits, elections are like striking gold for commercial media. Thanks to Citizens United, in which we, the people can also mean we, the corporations, more than 86 million campaign dollars[136] had flown from super PACs to media conglomerates as of March, 2012.

---

[132]2006. PBS Frontline. "Economic Reform and Political Repression: The Tank Man", (Antony Thomas Productions Ltd.), 13 April.

[133]Fenton, Tom. *Bad News: The Decline Of Reporting, The Business Of News, And The Danger To Us All,* (New York: Regan Books, c2005), p. 114.
[134]Moyers, Bill. *A Journalist And His Times,* (New York: New Press: Distributed by W. W. Norton, c2004) p. 130.
[135]2011.The Wall St. Journal under Rupert Murdoch. Pew Research Center. 20 July.
[136]2012. Super PAC Spending. Hitting $100 million in 2012. *BALLOTPEDIA.*
8 March. Available @ ballotpedia.org.

In his book *No Place To Hide*, Glen Greenwald writes:

> "The idea of a "fourth estate" is that those who exercise the greatest power need to be challenged by adversarial pushback and an insistence on transparency; the job of the press is to disprove the falsehoods that power invariably disseminates to protect itself. Without that type of journalism, abuse is inevitable."[137]

When leading scientists are trying to warn us, they should be heard. When an expert in commodities trading tries to sound an alarm over deregulation, her voice should not be silenced. When open and sound reporting is punished, or when demonstrators and peaceful protestors are video-taped, harassed and jailed we need to be informed.

When whistle blowing can be construed as a crime against a government, more flags of alarm should go up! A healthy democracy needs whistle blowers. It is the only way we can keep everyone honest. It is the only way we can be knowledgeable about the misdeeds of those who use wealth and power to keep us ignorant because what we don't know can, and does come back to bite us.

Fortunately, world citizens are not that willing to give up their right for full and open access to information. Today, every person with a portable internet device has the ability to video anything that captures their interest. It is no longer possible to remain ignorant of unjust conditions that occur anywhere on our planet. In this 21st century our new world of transparency is mirroring back the true condition of our societies.

Lights In The Darkness

Non-profit independent journalism, public TV, radio, and PEG local access cable broadcasts in cities all across America have been performing a great service to the public's need for information. It is a welcome alternative to commercial television's filtering and control of information, its race-to-the-bottom entertainment fare, and its endless commercials—as if our time is not valuable.

---

[137]Greenwald, Glen. N*o Place To Hide*. (New York: Metropolitan Books/Henry Holt, 2014). p. 230.

We should know what is going on in our names, especially when it contributes to a loss of respect for us in other countries around the world. How else can we, the public, take the measure of our leaders? Recent NSA exposures have been a catalyst in this developing paradigm of transparency, giving governments a new respect for our wired and interconnected world.

The writers of our American Constitution were keenly aware of the tremendous significance of public information. It was recognized early on by The First Amendment. America needs to achieve what the founding fathers originally envisioned for this country—a nation of informed citizens served by an ethical media that values integrity and full transparency.

As we enter this 21st century, our interconnected global internet is finally bringing this vision about!

CHAPTER THREE   WHOSE ECONOMY?

"Competition in the wild is a contest for survival in which the largest and strongest typically win.

Civilization, by contrast, is defined by rules; rules create markets, and governments generate the rules. ...Government doesn't "intrude" on the "free market". It creates the market."[138]

> \- Robert B. Reich, *Saving Capitalism For the Many, Not the Few.*

To accurately describe our world economy one needs to consider the term "externalities". Externalities can be thought of as a nice way of describing "victims " and the best way to approach the subject of externalities is to jump right in with examples.

If you look up the word *usury* in a dictionary you will find that it refers to interest in excess of a legal rate charged to a borrower for the use of money. In other words, exploitation of the borrower. This, thanks to the doing away with oversight and banking regulations, is what credit card companies did with customers and what bankers and mortgage brokers did to hundreds of thousands of Americans.

In the most recent housing and financial crisis, many of those borrowers were not just first-time home buyers; quite a few were on fixed incomes. They had already paid off their mortgages but needed to take out a second mortgage to keep up the maintenance of their homes.

---

[138]Reich, Robert B. *Saving Capitalism For the Many, Not the Few,* (New York: Alfred A. Knopf, 2015) p.4.

Bad loans that were quickly packaged into collateralized debt obligations (CDOs), became the latest Wall Street craze and were sold to the highest bidders. This resulted in cash heaped into the lending banks' coffers, enabling them to turn around and secure even more bad sub-prime mortgages. Finally, when those annual percentage rates (APRs) leaped, and borrowers could not meet their suddenly escalating mortgage payments, these same CDO packages suddenly turned into worthless investments. Global speculators, big banks, and Wall Street were left with no place to drop them.[139]

But were these profit-driven financial institutions to be left helpless? Were they expected to take their losses and learn from their misbehavior? Was anyone prosecuted and sent to jail? Certainly not. In order to save our economy, our tax money had to come to their rescue.

You might wonder, however, where was the money to bail out all those homeowners whose homes were lost, all those investors whose pension funds were compromised, and because row after row of home foreclosures with their barred-up windows, vandalized buildings, decaying neighborhoods, packed homeless shelters, and food banks, do not constitute an adequate real-estate tax base, mayors and city governments across the country found there was no money coming in to handle their civic obligations.

Similar to the plight of American workers caused by the exodus of middle-class jobs to lower-wage countries as a result of multi-national trade agreements, local governments became the "externalities" of the bailed-out banking industry.

The state of California is a good example. In the August 2009 issue of *The Nation,* Marc Cooper described California as a "Failed State"[140] Paychecks were being replaced by IOUs, teachers were going on hunger strikes, thousands of state employees had been laid off, some of the state parks were no longer open to Californians, and its bond rating was downgraded to near-junk status.

Chapter Three   Whose Economy?

[139]Phillips,Kevin. *Bad Money: Reckless Finance, Failed Politics, And The Global Crisis of American Capitalism,* (New York: Viking, 2008), pp. 3, 35, 36.
[140]Cooper, Marc. 2009. "Letter From A State In Crisis". *The Nation.* August, p. 13.

Cooper noted that southern California had its highest peak in personal bankruptcies in that year—up 75 percent, and one in four capsized mortgages in the United States was in California."[141]

The damaging externalities of this latest financial crisis have included not just home foreclosures all across our country, but also renters, local businesses, and communities whose city governments lost the funds needed to support schools, public works infrastructure, public libraries, police, and firemen.

Remember the Enron crisis? Before the sub-prime mortgage debacle, Enron, in 2000, was actively removing restrictive regulations on their futures contracts.[142] The blackouts in California were the direct result of this deregulation. For weeks we heard news of California's escalating electricity costs and energy shortages due to Enron's secret auctions. Not only California residents, but the shareholders and employees of Enron were the externalities of that deregulation strategy.

The Externalities of Warfare

Warfare has always been an extremely profitable activity. But for each dollar of profit made, millions of unfortunate men, women, and children living in war zones as well as thousands of American service men and women along with their children, pay with their lives, their homes, their physical and mental health, and their lost futures. The unequaled 2015 mass refugee crisis escaping the violence and destruction in Syria, Iraq, Yemen, Afghanistan, and Africa is a good example of the evil consequences of war.

However, since these human externalities do not show up on corporate profit and loss statements, war continues to be a good business model. The more weapons needed, the greater the inventory turnover. The more infrastructure destroyed, the greater the need for new structures to be built by corporate construction companies and the more a failed state goes into debt, the greater the wealth accrues to a hedge fund.

---

[141]Ibid.
[142]California electricity crisis. Wikipedia, the free encyclopedia.

Warfare also adds great profits to chemical industries. Chemical and biological agents have played leading roles not only in two world wars but in Vietnam, and the Middle East. Warfare also adds a steady stream of income to drug manufacturers; there is a great demand for anti-depressants and pain killers by the military. As of 2007, "about 12% of combat troops in Iraq and 17% of those in Afghanistan" were taking prescription antidepressants or sleeping pills.[143]

Prozac, Zoloft, and Ambien may help to numb the experience of horror on the battlefield, but numbing the mind is just a temporary fix. And, what is not visible is the negative energy generated in populations as a result of war, thus insuring a future inflow of even more profits for the war industry in the next outbreak of violence.

The Cost-Benefit Analysis

In 2005, General Motors decided not to change a defective ignition switch redesign because it would have added about a dollar to the cost of each car. As a result of this decision at least over 124 people have died due to faulty switches.[144] In order to prevent criminal prosecution, GM agreed to pay $900 million to the government, which is really just a tiny amount of the $50 billion of tax money used to bail out GM in 2009.

By this bailout, the government became a 60% GM shareholder. Yet, during the following years nothing was done to require GM to report defects in their cars to the Center for Auto Safety.[145]

GM knew about this problem, even changed the switch without changing the part number in order to cover it up for more than a decade. To add further insult, those motorists who suffered crashes due to the defective ignition switch, were

---

[143]Thompson, Mark. 2008. "America's Medicated Army". *Time*, 171, no. 24. p. 39.
[144]2015."UPDATE 3-U.S. weighs charges against GM over ignition switch recall –WSJ." REUTERS. 9 June. reuters.com/article/2015/06/09/gm-probe-
[145]2015. GM Did the Crime, Drivers Do the Time: Ralph Nader on Failure of U.S. to Prosecute Car Executives. *"Democracy Now-The War and Peace Report"*. 18, September Available @ democracynow.org.

charged with vehicular manslaughter, yet no one at GM will be charged for a crime.[146]

But this isn't the only time a GM cost analysis took precedence over a human life. In his book, *The Corporation,* Joel Bakan writes of what happened to a mother and her four children on Christmas Day in 1993. After being rear-ended while waiting for a red light to change, they found themselves in a flaming automobile. Three children had over 60 percent of their bodies burned and one lost her hand.

As Bakan explains, General Motors, in an effort to cut down on costs, placed the fuel tank 6 inches closer to the rear bumper and did away with the metal brace that separates the fuel tank from the rear of the car. But GM suffered no lasting penalties because by keeping their costs down they were just acting in support of their shareholders, therefore it was all perfectly legal.[147]

So you see, the company was only following the law even if that meant putting someone's life at risk. Our system of justice has given the corporation the same status as a human being, but even a human being is not allowed to put a human life in danger!

Profit as Law

Here is the root problem. As Bakan explains, once a corporation goes public, it is legally obliged to maximize shareholder wealth.[148] The key word here is *legally*; corporate profit maximization is protected under law. In effect, this means that because a corporation is a steward of other people's money, it is illegal for a corporation to ignore a cost analysis. As a result, corporations do get away with murder. This is what has allowed multi-national corporations to go into undeveloped countries and ravage them, all under the guise of free-trade.

---

[146]Ibid.
[147]Bakan, Joel. *The Corporation: The Pathological Pursuit Of Profit And Power*, (New York: c2004), pp. 75-79.

[148]Ibid.

To further explore Milton Friedman's concept of an *externality*, it can be a harmful occurrence that happens to someone or something as a result of a corporation's irresponsible *legal* activity, the bottom line is, it's someone else's problem—not the corporation's. Their only responsibility is to make a profit.

Smoke, Smoke, Smoke That Cigarette

Victims of the cigarette industry are another good example of externalities. Had it not been for Dr. Jeffrey Wigand, who as Vice-President for Research and Development at Brown and Williamson Tobacco Corporation, blew the whistle on the tobacco industry's denial of nicotine's addictive properties, this industry would still be delivering the deadly poison nicotine to unaware Americans today.[149] As has already been noted, so often the actions of just one conscientious person can take down the mightiest of institutions.

As this demonstrates, the priority of profit over the welfare of human beings is a major problem that too often goes unexposed unless there is a whistle blower willing to put his or her life and career on the line.

Sex Externalities

There's nothing like a major economic disaster or a failed state to make promiscuity extremely profitable. All across the globe sex trafficking increases whenever an economy is under attack. Victims become entrapped at a very young age. In the magazine, *Foreign Policy,* David Feingold writes of the prevalence of beatings, sexual assault, unpaid labor, sleep deprivation, and rape of Burmese domestic workers in Thailand. He notes that the 2005 U.S. government figures indicated the presence of some "200,000 trafficked victims in the United States."[150]

In 1998 when the Russian economy collapsed, and hundreds of millions of Russians had a total of $500 billion in cash stolen from them by Russian

---

[149]1996. Jeffrey Wigand on 60 Minutes. 4 February. jeffreywigand.com/60minutes.php
[150]Feingold, David A., 2005. Think Again Human Trafficking. *Foreign Policy,* September/October.

oligarchs,[151] sex-trafficking for the benefit of wealthy investors became a perk of the new Russian economy. Fourteen year-old girls, just like Thailand's domestic workers, had become the new externalities in Russia's lucrative sex trade.

As powerful multi-national corporations move in on a country and drain it of its economic resources, or as more and more countries become decimated by warfare, more and more trafficked victims become externalities in the lucrative sex-trade.

Health Care

Externalities in the health care industry are legion. Medical bills have been found to be the number one cause of bankruptcy and homelessness in the United States. As our nation grapples with the ridiculously spiraling cost of medical care and health insurance, lobbyists are diligent in their fight to prevent the threat of any kind of public option.

Michael Moore's film, "Sicko" painted a very revealing picture of how our extremely expensive health-care system ranked 37th in the world when compared with health care in other countries.[152]

He explains the importance of understanding that even non-profits are actually all about making huge profits; we are not to be fooled by promises of universal coverage. It doesn't mean a thing if it is not a government single-payer program.[153]

Whatever You Do To The Least Of These. . .

In a Democracy Now 2007 interview with Andy Bales of the Union Rescue Mission in Los Angeles, Bales told of patients that have been removed from hospitals, put into cabs and dropped off in skid row. In Los Angeles there had been more than 35 drop-offs. He noted approximately 11 hospitals were doing this. Some were dumped off with an IV still in their arms![154]

---

[151]Ruppert, Michael C. *Crossing The Rubicon*, (Gabriola Island, B.C.: New Society Publishers, c 2004), pp. 91-93.
[152]Moore, Michael. 2007. *Free Speech TV, "Democracy Now-The War and Peace Report"*, discussion with Michael Moore, 14 June. Available @ democracynow.org.
[153]Ibid.
[154]Bales, Andy. 2007. discussion with Andy Bales of the Union Rescue Mission, Los Angeles. *Free Speech TV, "Democracy Now-The War and Peace Report"*. 14 June. Available @ democracynow.org.

In the drug industry, television commercials offering the industry's latest drugs to solve the problems of obesity, impotence, sleep deprivation, cholesterol, and depression, etc. bombard us daily. Yet, the tragedy of millions in our world who suffer untold agonies as they die daily from disease and warfare, points out how one market increases the bottom line, the other doesn't. As Joel Bakan points out, poverty stricken countries are only 20% of the global market for drugs.[155]

Draining A Country

In *Confessions of an Economic Hit Man*, author John Perkins gives us a thorough picture of how politically effective it is to get the leader of a country to take out huge development loans which can never be repaid. This is accomplished by promising the leader and his or her family great wealth, thereby guaranteeing obedience from them, but poverty for the rest of that county's population. These communities wind up with leaders that do not represent their interests, loans they cannot repay, children they cannot feed, schools they cannot build, and water they cannot drink. Perkins described how all across the planet, the leaders of third-world countries signed on with economic hit men. He should know, as he was once an economic hit-man himself.[156]

And in *The Shock Doctrine,* author Naomi Klein chronicles how effective has been the practice of Milton Friedman's Chicago School of free-trade economics.[157] She describes how neo-liberal or neo-conservative economists have managed to rape the wealth from every country they subdue. First, the country is shocked into total helplessness ("disaster capitalism"), either by a natural disaster like a tsunami, a coup, or by deliberate economic manipulation.

Some effective methods used to increase economic disaster can include union breaking, massive layoffs and firings, deregulation, major price increases on basic needs like food, gas, water and transportation, and foreign takeover of all the

---

[155]Bakan, Joel. *The Corporation: The Pathological Pursuit Of Profit And Power*, (New York: Free Press, c2004), p. 49.
[156]Perkins, John. *Confessions of an Economic Hit Man*, (San Francisco, CA: Berrett-Koehler, c2004).
[157]Klein, Naomi. *The Shock Doctrine: The Rise of Disaster Capitalism*, (New York: Metropolitan Books/ Henry Holt, 2007).

country's natural resources resulting in a total financial drain from the country's local economy.[158]

Greece struggles to survive an austerity program to pay a $320 billion debt.[159] As of 2015 the people have been living under this program for five years and the despair is extremely high. It must either continue with the enforced austerity program to repay its debt or withdraw from the Euro Zone.

To Greece's citizens, continuing with austerity means an increase in the already 50 percent male suicides, an increase in the already 25 percent drop in real wages in five years, and an increase in the already 15 percent of people who cannot afford health care.[160]

However, to hedge funds, by hiking the interest rate on Greece's already high debt, austerity means squeezing Greece of even more of its dollars, thereby filling the hedge fund's coffers with even more of their already ill-gotten wealth for years to come[161] Meanwhile this makes it impossible for Greece to ever pay down its debt.

And when this happens, the field is left wide open for far-right political groups to step in and exploit the frustration and anger of those victims of austerity. This happened in Germany with the Nazi Party and can possibly happen again in Greece with the far-right party, Golden Dawn.   And if Puerto Rico cannot be given a way to deal with its economic collapse, that same scenario may play out.

Disaster Capitalism

Regarding free-trade interventionist policies, Naomi Klein describes. how unethical leaders who take out huge IMF loans to cover their debt are required to allow foreign corporations to erect dams, build plants, and construct infrastructure

[158]Ibid.
[159]2015. *Free Speech TV, "Democracy Now-The War and Peace Report"*, Rejecting Austerity, Greece Squares off with its Creditors & Risks Future in Eurozone. 18, February. Available @ democracynow.org.
[160]Ibid.
[161]Foley, Stephen and Savaricas, Nathalie. 'Vulture Funds' Circle as Greece Fears Grow.17 May. independent.co.uk/news/business/news/vulture-funds-circle-as-greece-fears-grow-758127.html

that gouges the environment.[162] Foreign banks move in and drain the country of its money. The country's rivers are polluted, its forests are cut down, and its people are exploited.

Should citizens be so bold as to protest, Klein notes that the next tool used to squelch their opposition is torture and kidnapping. In many cases mutilated bodies have been left in public places to further intimidate the population.[163] She explains how many free-trade interventionist policies in Latin America, Mexico, Africa, the Middle East, Indonesia, the Pacific Ring countries, and Asia have betrayed our good name.

Policies such as vulture capitalism, deregulation, escalating food prices, and loss of jobs have produced shantytowns, little or no educational opportunity for children, deterioration of infrastructure, human rights violations, and rape of the environment.[164]

Victims have included Mexico, Poland, Russia, Trinidad, Tobego, Indonesia, Thailand, South Korea, Sri Lanka, India, China, the Philippines, and countries in Latin and Central America.[165]

Buying Up America –ALEC

And now, here in America, we too are getting a taste of this disaster capitalism that has profited the 1% wealthy elite at the expense of the rest of us. As a result of the Supreme Court's 2010 decision in Citizens United v. Federal Election Commission, under the guise of free speech, shadowy groups can now pump many millions of dollars into our federal and state election campaigns.[166]

The successful influence of ALEC (American Legislative Executive Council), is funded by wealthy extreme right-wing conservatives. It focuses on influencing

---

[162]Klein, Naomi. *The Shock Doctrine: The Rise of Disaster Capitalism*, (New York: Metropolitan Books/ Henry Holt, 2007).
[163]Ibid. pp. 15, 16.
[164]Ibid.
[165]Ibid, pp. 276, 277..
[166]2012. Dunbar, John. The 'Citizens United' decision and why it matters. The Center for Public Integrity. 18 October.

state lawmakers to enact new laws to further weaken public services, unions, and basic human rights.[167]

It is interesting that ALEC prefers to keep its membership secret. ALEC works on state houses across the country to advance its corporate agenda of benefiting corporate profit over public policy. Lawmakers are wined and dined in luxurious locations and given "suggestions" which then show up as new bills like *"Stand Your Ground"* in Florida which weakens our justice system; *"weakening of collective bargaining rights"* in Wisconsin which go after unions that have built up America's middle-class; *"improving education"* in North Carolina and Tennessee which drains public education budgets, *"taxpayer money allocated for ALEC attendance"* in South Dakota which uses public funds to cover travel expenses of state legislators; and *"attempts to weaken North Carolina's renewable energy standard"* again in North Carolina.[168]

Richmond, CA v. Chevron

Without the counter-balancing force of a strong and ethical government, corporations have no restrictions on their activity and the public along with our planet, loses. However, there are grassroots success stories. For example, Chevron, a Fortune 500 company, was guilty of negligence at its Richmond, CA refinery in the Bay area. After a history of fires, the city's Mayor, Gayle McLaughlin, sued Chevron. The company retaliated by spending over three million dollars in a flood of attack ads against Richmond's progressive candidates in the November, 2014 election.

But the voters were not fooled. Chevron lost. Voters supported their progressive candidates anyway and after votes were counted, every progressive candidate won! Not only that, but the city is collecting two hundred million dollars from Chevron to improve its citizens' living conditions.[169]

---

[167]*Moyers & Company*. 2013. Investigating ALEC, The American Legislative Executive Council. 21 June. Available @ billmoyers.com
[168]*Moyers & Company*. 2013. Tracking the ALEC Law-Making Machine. 30 May. Available @ billmoyers.com.
[169]Ibid., 2014. Facing Down Corporate Election Greed. 7 November.

The Corporation Becomes Protected

In 1886 the corporate form was given the same status as a natural person under the law, allowing it to became constitutionally protected from the rest of us. The Supreme Court declared this in the *Santa Clara v. Southern Pacific Railroad Co.* case thereby subordinating the people's sovereignty to the large corporation.[170]

But a corporation is an institution in which all its members and shareholders do not necessarily hold the same ideals. Neither is it an organic living, breathing, human being. It does not blush, cry, suffer, bleed, go to jail, or die. A corporation can buy many friends. But in the human universe, friendship and love are not for sale. The two can never be put on the same footing. Yet, the corporation is protected by law as if it were.

This travesty of justice has been continuing right up to today. *Citizens United*, in which the Supreme Court in January 2010, gave corporations the same protections as citizens in using their funds to finance elections, is the most recent example of inequality.[171] And it is all perfectly legal!

Corporations have been able to increase their dominance over us until they control every aspect of our society. As a result, national and international banks as well as corporate executives are doing extremely well in our world economy, thank you very much. Unfortunately, the environment and the rest of the population are not.

America's Externalities

Here in America an increasing number of middle-class workers for whom home ownership, health insurance, and a higher education have become a luxury, must work harder for longer hours just to keep from losing their low-paying jobs and falling into even greater poverty. Young people are increasingly crushed by rising student loans. As of 2014 total student debt had reached $1.1 trillion.[172] This is

---

[170]Coleridge, Greg. 2001. March Of Folly. Corporate Perversion of the Fourteenth Amendment. P. 106. Included in: *Defying Corporations, Defining Democracy, A Book Of History & Strategy*. Edited by Dean Ritz. (New York: Apex Press, 2001), p. 106.

[171]*Citizens United v. FEC. Wikipedia, the free encyclopedia.*

[172]Quandt, Katie Rose. 2015. "Money in Politics Is Darkening the Future for Millenials." *Moyers & Company. billmoyers.com.*

what happens when the student loan industry can spend $4.5 million dollars to keep college interest rates high.[173]

Senator Elizabeth Warren points out how the federal government loan rate of only 0.75 % for big Wall St. banks shows how big banks are valued over students.[174] But a country that devalues its students is a country that dooms itself to ignorance, dysfunction, and eventually, a failed-state status.

In fact, more and more families with children struggle with unemployment, low wages, credit card debt, high medical costs, repossessions, and home foreclosures.

The city of Detroit is a good example. In debt for $5 billion, because it lost most of its tax base, its public services have been going without funding. Infrastructure has been decaying. Wages have dropped.

"The poverty rate is approximately 40 percent and people have seen their water bills increase by 119 percent within the last decade."[175] On top of this, the Detroit Water and Sewerage Department began turning off the taps of those whose bills were above $150. Thousands of residential account holders have had their tap water shut off, two-thirds of whom are families with children. But water, like air, is absolutely necessary for survival.

Meera Karunananthan, member of the Blue Planet Project, which authored an appeal to the United Nations over this violation of human rights, compared the city of Detroit's average monthly water bill of around $75 per month with the national average monthly water bill of between $40 and $50. And now, she noted that for a family of four, they're paying $150 to $200 per month, up 20 percent— another example of the economic concept of "externalities".[176]

Increasing Private Takeover Of All Things Public

In addition to the bottled-water industry capturing our public water resources, prisons turn out to be another profitable business venture. Private prisons bring in

---

[173]Ibid.
[174]Ibid.
[175]2014. Free Speech TV, *"Democracy Now-The War and Peace Report"*, Water is a Human Right: Detroit Residents Seek U.N. Intervention as City Shuts Off Water Taps to Thousands. 24 June. Available @ democracynow.org.
[176]Ibid.

billions of dollars in profits. Of course, the more prisoners a for-profit jail has the more profit it makes! A recent scandalous development involved former Pennsylvania Juvenile Court Judge Mark Ciavarella, Jr. who took more than $2.6 million in kickbacks for sending teenagers to privately-run detention centers. Five thousand juveniles were the externalities in this scheme.[177]

America keeps more people behind bars than the top European countries combined. It has 5 percent of the world's population but 25 percent of the world's prisoners; from 500,000 prisoners in 1980 to 2.2 million prisoners in 2015.[178]

The proportion of black and brown prisoners far exceeds the rest of America's prison population. And since detained immigrants, poor and marginalized citizens (including teenagers) cannot afford the luxury of effective legal representation, poverty, racism, and immigration increase the wealth for the profit-driven prison industry.

Cashing In On Immigrant Women and Children

Calling conditions in these privately-run prisons "deplorable", U.S. District Judge Dolly Gee gave the Obama administration 90 days either to release the more than 2,000 women and children being held in two Texas facilities or show just cause to continue holding them.[179]

In describing the Karnes and Dilley detention centers, Rep. Judy Chu was shocked and very moved by the desperate pleas of hundreds of mothers who said they are not criminals and want to be released. Barbara Hines, a longtime immigration lawyer with many clients who are detained in these detention centers points out that children cannot legally be housed in secured, unlicensed facilities that have no independent oversight and are kept away from their parents.[180]

Texas judges have started ordering mothers' and children's' release without bond, but the only way ICE will allow mothers to be released, is to force them to

---

[177]Urbina, Ian and Hamill, Sean D. 2009. The New York Times, 12 February.
[178]2015. Strange Bedfellows:Why are the Kock Brothers and Van Jones Teeming Up to End Mass Incarceration? 15 July. Available @ democracynow.org.
[179]2015. "Deplorable": Federal Judge Condemns For-Profit Detention Centers For Immigrant Families. 29 July. Available @ democracynow.org.
[180]Ibid.

wear tight ankle shackles which cause their legs to swell up, making them appear to be prisoners, and putting their children through trauma.

These shackles are made by the BI Company which was bought out by GEO, one of the private companies that run these detention centers.[181] So profits are realized, not just by running private detention centers but also by providing supplies like shackles, for its prisoners.

It is ludicrous to refer to these centers as family detention centers, when it is really a jail-like coercive environment that isolates parents from their children. These mothers and children are asylum seekers fleeing rape and violence in Central America and private interests are capitalizing on their misfortune.

The Safe Justice Act

Supported by both Democrats and Republicans, the Safe Justice Act would end the huge explosion rate of America's high incarceration rate by 50 percent over the next ten years.[182]

The vast majority of nonviolent prisoners will eventually be released. The goal is to rehabilitate, give job training, "Ban The Box" by removing the disclosure requirement on job applications, restore their right to vote, and correct this abusive punitive justice system.

Laws like mandatory minimums, three strikes you're out, truth in sentencing laws, abusive prosecutorial misconduct, and privatizing the prison industry to create private for-profit prisons, have all worked to create this high incarceration rate.

Calling for an overhaul of a justice system that he refers to as "broken", President Barack Obama became the first sitting president in history to visit a federal prison.[183] On July 13,2015 he granted clemency to 46 men and women facing extreme sentences (including life in prison) for nonviolent drug offenses.

---

[181]Ibid.
[182]Ibid.
[183]Ibid. 2015. . Free Speech TV, *"Democracy Now-The War and Peace Report"* 17 July.

Commenting on prison reform, Maya Schenwar, author of *Locked Down, Locked Out: Why Prison Doesn't Work and How We Can Do Better,* points out that prison reform is a good start, but it shouldn't stop there.[184]

Transitioning non-violent offenders back to society should recognize that putting them on electronic monitors, sending them to a locked-down drug treatment facility or locked-down mental health facility, only recreates a prison environment. And excluding from prison reform a huge number of people who have been convicted of violent offenses, disregards the fact that racism, and economic violence are at the root cause.

She believes we must be careful about how we re-channel the $80 billion we would save by decarcerating people. To redirect it into so-called "public safety measures" that only heighten policing puts that money right back into the same problem. Instead, she suggests that we would do much better by reinvesting in early childhood education, mental healthcare, or community resources.[185]

Solitary Confinement

Any prison reform must also include ending the cruel and inhumane practice of solitary confinement. California keeps nearly 3,000 prisoners alone for more than 22 hours a day in windowless cells, with no human contact. Some prisoners have been held like this for decades.

Throughout the country about 80,000 people are in solitary confinement, many of whom are in for minor offenses or are just mentally ill.[186] As a result of litigation put forward by California Families to Abolish Solitary Confinement, the state of California has agreed to greatly reduced this barbaric practice.
Jules Lobel, attorney representing prisoners at Pelican Bay sees this as a model for prisons across America.[187]

---

[184]Ibid. 2015. Discussion with Maya Schenwar, editor-in-chief of Truthout and author of *Locked Down, Locked Out:* Why Prison Doesn't Work and How We Can Do Better. 17 July.
[185]Ibid.
[186]2015. Free Speech TV, *"Democracy Now-The War and Peace Report"* "After Mass Hunger Strikes & Lawsuits, Prisoners Force California to Scale Back Solitary Confinement. 2 September.

[187]Ibid.

Solitary Confinement's Effect on Juveniles

Since juveniles brains and bodies are still in the developing stage, keeping them in isolation does great damage to their mental health.

A case in point is Kalif Browder, a 16-year old African American teenager in New York who was sent to Rikers Island prison for stealing a backpack despite his insistence that he was innocent. He even refused an offer of freedom if he would admit to being guilty. So he was kept in prison for three years (two of which were in solitary confinement). After he was eventually released, his experience of isolation and brutal treatment by the prison guards left him so psychologically damaged that he took his own life.[188]

Because so many juveniles (17,000)[189] are kept in isolation, a bill calling for prohibition of solitary confinement for juveniles in the federal system has been introduced in the U.S. Senate.

Profiting From Education Reform

With little oversight or accountability, the education reform movement including charter schools which enjoys privileges that public schools do not, provides an opportunity for "cashing in on kids" while at the same time draining public funds.

Wall St. hedge funds have been quick to recognize this school reform movement as another new profit-making activity. Michael Moe, a veteran of Lehman Brothers and Merrill Lynch, sees the education reform movement as the next big "undercapitalized" sector of the economy.[190] The charter school movement is also being promoted by the Walton Family Foundation to the tune of hundreds of millions of dollars—another example of how a public service is being taken over by immense wealth.[191]

---

[188]2015. Free Speech TV, *"Democracy Now-The War and Peace Report"*, Strange Bedfellows:Why are the Koch Brothers and Van Jones Teeming Up to End Mass Incarceration? 15 July. Available @ democracynow.org.

[189]Williams, Timothy. 2015. In Solitary at 14: The Risks of Isolation. *Times Digest*. 16 August.

[190]2011. Fang, Lee. "Selling Schools Out". The Scam of Virtual Education Reform. The Nation. 5 December.

[191]cashinginon kids.com/?page_id=1520

National Parks

Our national parks are also coming under attack by private interests. The Koch-backed Property and Environment Research Center (PERC) and its oil and gas allies are working to give public lands back to the states, knowing that since states would not have enough funds to manage these lands they would have to be sold off to the highest bidder—thus, opening up these lands to more oil drilling and mining operations.[192]

An Unjust Economic System

Through a process called inversion, corporations, CEOs, and banks, make billions of dollars by faking a false address in a different country, leaving their tax burdens for the rest of America's citizens. Nobel Prize Winning-economist, Joseph Stiglitz, gives examples of some of the biggest tax dodgers in 2012.[193]

He cites how Citigroup, by keeping its profits of $42.6 billion dollars offshore, was able to pay no taxes. Exxon Mobile in 2012, had $43 billion in profits offshore in 2012 and it paid no taxes. Also, General Electric made $88 billion from 2002 to 2012 and paid just 2.4 percent in taxes for a tax subsidy of $29 billion.[194]

Referring to this as moral treason, Stiglitz says,

> "We have become a house divided against itself—divided between
> the 99 percent and the 1 percent, between the workers and those who
> would exploit them. We have to reunite the house..."[195]

In *Perfectly Legal,* author David Cay Johnston writes:

> "The most important measure of tax burden is how many pennies
> out of each dollar go to taxes. The top 400 taxpayers in 2000 had an
> average income of $174 million, yet they paid just 22 cents on the dollar
> in federal income taxes.
> ...Had the 2003 tax cuts been in effect, the top 400 would have paid just
> 17.5 cents on the dollar, not much more than the overall national average of
> 15.3 cents that Americans actually paid that year."[196]

---

[192]nationofchange.org/2015/3/17/the-quiet-plan-to-sell-off-americas-national-forests/
[193]*Bill Moyers and Company*. 2014. Encore interview with Nobel Prize-winning economist, Joseph E. Stiglitz, "Fair Taxes For All". 21 August. Available @ billmoyers.com
[194]Ibid.
[195]Ibid.
[196]Johnston, David Cay. *Perfectly Legal,* (New York:Portfolio, c2003), pp.306-308.

In America, a Wall Street CEO's yearly income is in the millions of dollars a year yet only pays a social security tax on up to $250,000 of that income. Not so for average Americans who are taxed on every penny of their wages. And of course, CEO salaries are considered a business expense which automatically reduces corporate tax obligations.

One could question how such an unjust society has evolved in a country that for so long has been predominantly Christian. Christians are supposed to care for one another, but in the lives of many so-called Christians we see a total rejection of the message of the prophets who were always concerned with an unjust social system. But for many, grace seems to be synonymous with power and money.

How comforting to believe that because you profess to be a saved Christian, you are not only guaranteed salvation, but you do not have to be overly concerned about social injustice.

Regarding the recent embrace of church and politics in America, Cornel West, in his book, *Democracy Matters,* points out that it is not a new phenomenon, nor is it an accident, and it most definitely is not a spiritual awakening![197]

It is easy to understand a church's zeal to identify with members who are a steady source of income and how easy to understand a candidate's zeal for a religion which promises to clinch an election.

How hypocritical is it to wax eloquent about the need to do away with government, while at the same time using government to increase your private wealth? How moral is it to make a charitable contribution to be used as good PR and a tax write-off, yet withhold the well-being from another?

Interesting, isn't it, that when the minimum wage was ever so slightly increased by Congress, a big bonus of $20 billion dollars in tax breaks to wealthy corporations was quietly sneaked in.[198] Raising the minimum wage by $2 and then giving tax relief in the billions to the wealthy would seem a bit skewed to even the most dull-witted.

[197]West, Cornel. *Democracy Matters, Winning the Fight Against Imperialism,* (New York: The Penguin Press, 2004).
[198]Moyers, Bill. *Moyers on America: A Journalist And His Times,* (New York: New Press: Distributed by W. W. Norton, c2004), p. 65.

Those who say Jesus is their hero and yet benefit by the largesse of generous government support at the expense of ordinary taxpayers are fooling themselves. Claiming to be saved doesn't mean an awful lot if it means conveniently gaining by the exploitation of one's fellowman.

The poor are not fooled by our hypocrisy. This was described beautifully in a metaphor used by Father Schumacher, a priest who worked with the poor in Chicago. He made the obvious point in describing this emotional distance from the poor with an analogy: "What young lady would take a lover seriously who made his proposal by mail, money order enclosed?"[199]

Wealth is not proof that God is on your side just as poverty is not an indication that God is not. We are all—rich and poor—animated by the same impartial invisible life force. Jesus and the prophets didn't play favorites. The demand for justice is not so much for a hand-out as it is for a just society in which there is no need for a hand-out—a society where wealth is not obtained by causing externalities.

---

[199]Facchini, Rocco A. and Daniel J. *Muldoon: A True Chicago Ghost Story, Tales of a Forgotten Rectory*, (Chicago: Lake Claremont Press 2003), p. 244.

CHAPTER FOUR   SHADES OF DEMOCRACY

"When 32 people can outspend 3.7 million citizens, our democracy is in real danger."[200]

-Senator Elizabeth Warren

It's All About Your Contacts

Capitol Hill experience can be a ticket to wealth! It's no secret that there is a revolving door between Washington and corporate interests. In fact, working as a lobbyist can eventually increase the salary of a retired lawmaker by over 1400 percent. Bidding for a retired house member starts at $500,000 and at a million dollars for a retired senator.[201]

In *Demosclerosis,* author Jonathan Rauch noted that according to *Congress Daily/A.M.*, fully 40 percent of the House of Representatives members who left office in January 1993 went to work as lobbyists for international corporations.[202] This phenomenon is popularly referred to as the revolving door.

Targeting Regulation

Lobbyists represent huge international corporate wealth and they have chaired both the Republican and Democratic National Committees. They re-write our laws by purchasing the allegiance of our elected officials. Their major focus is to remove laws and regulations that decrease their corporate profits.

Chapter Four   Shades of Democracy

[200] www.warren.senate.gov/?p=press_release&id=611
[201] republicreport.org/2012/make-it-rain-revolving-door/
[202] Rauch, Jonathan. *Demosclerosis: The Silent Killer of American Government,* (New York: Times Books, c1994), p. 88.

Regulatory agencies began to feel this sting in the mid-1990s when Newt Gingrich and huge business contributions entered the scene.[203] As lobbyists, these prior congressmen could now use their formerly gained political expertise to aim for the right people in Washington.

In *Moyers on America,* Bill Moyers noted: "By 2004, the cost to each taxpayer for the corrupting activities of these lobbyists has been estimated at $1,600 per year."[204] This exposes how the power of wealth to influence a market economy's rules benefits corporations at the expense of working Americans.

Consider commercial media. How many of us had a chance to weigh in on the 1996 media consolidation when the FCC gave away public air rights to private corporations?

Elections are another case in point. Long before any election is held, big money, thanks to Citizens United, has already decided who will run. In our democracy, all branches of government are dependent for their survival on corporate campaign contributions, lobbying, and special interests. Instead of honest dialogue with their constituents, too many leaders engage in deception, reputation smearing, and strategies of spin.

According to an article in the January 26, 2015 edition of the *New York Times,* the Koch brothers who are among the wealthiest in America, plan to spend $889 million on the 2016 election—more than President Obama spent on his entire re-election campaign and almost double what Mitt Romney spent in 2012.[205]

Do average Americans have money like that?

And because the Kochs oppose any campaign disclosure, their expansive network of non-profit advocacy groups (that nevertheless, have definite political intent), allow them to keep their donors and activities hidden.

---

[203]Sirota, David. 2006. "Newt's New Con." *The Nation.* 30 January.

[204]Moyers, Bill. *Moyers on America: A Journalist And His Times,* (New York: New Press: Distributed by W. W. Norton, c2004), p. 73.
[205]Confessore, Nicholas. 2015. Koch Brothers' Budget of $889 Million for 2016. *The New York Times.* 26 January.

Treating American Communities as War Zones

In America, protections given by our constitution that we have often taken for granted, have already been disappearing right under our noses. Even the Posse Comitatus Act, which prevents the military from engaging in domestic law enforcement, has eroded. For example, in 1980, only 20% of towns had SWAT (Special Weapons And Tactics) teams. But by 2005 the number of towns with SWAT teams had risen to 80%.[206]

Across America, police departments in small towns like Keene, NH (population 23,000), Cullman County, Alabama (population 14,000), Ferguson, Missouri (population 21,000), Post Falls, Idaho (population 28,000), and High Springs, Florida (population 5,350) have been receiving armored tanks, automatic military-style weapons, tear gas and gas masks, body armor, drones, and Bear Cats with large military-style rifles attached.[207]

It makes you wonder what possible threats to the American citizenry could be in these towns that would necessitate an occupying arsenal.

Rights like freedom from unreasonable searches (Stop and Frisk), privacy (NSA eavesdropping and data collection), free speech (gag laws and national security letters), freedom of association (spying on Wal-Mart union attempts and Occupy demonstrations), access to information (lack of government transparency), and legal representation requiring a speedy and public trial (extraordinary rendition, and Guantanamo), are rights that are vital to a democracy. But anyone who thinks democracy is possible without constant diligence, needs to think again.

Lessons of the Great Depression

Some of us can remember our grandparents describing how difficult were the depression years in America. The tragic suffering was nation-wide. To get a clear picture of just how serious was this depression, President Roosevelt sent journalists out across the nation to report back to him on what they found. They were instructed to get as much information as they were able.

[206] Rosenfeld, Steven. When Did Americans Become The Enemy? Available @ alternet.org
[207] Ibid.

What they came back with was a haunting picture of despair in our democratic Republic. In her book, *Gellhorn: A Twentieth Century Life,* Caroline Moorehead, recounts how Martha Gellhorn, a foreign correspondent in Europe during the events leading up to and through World War II, was one of those journalists.[208]

Dispatched to the New England area, Martha was appalled at the condescension and misuse of power she saw in the administration of public relief. She was barely able to get over her own personal depression at the sight of syphilis, smallpox, starvation and fear, that was everywhere she looked.[209] She couldn't believe that such conditions existed here in this civilized country. President Roosevelt got this same message from other journalists as well.

Finally, in 1934, instead of ignoring the pain as followers of Milton Friedman's Free-Trade Economics Chicago School would advise, he created the New Deal along with regulatory reforms and programs to restore the nation back to health. He was rightly convinced that the private business community would never step up to the plate; governmental action was the only hope for the country to get back on its feet. But by his action, President Roosevelt earned himself new enemies.

An Attempt at Fascism

There has always been a symbiotic relationship between Wall Street and the Military Industrial Complex; it didn't just begin with the Vietnam or the Iraq war and Roosevelt's New Deal threatened this relationship. In order to gain back control of government, an unholy alliance between the military and wealthy financiers was formed.

Joel Bakan describes how major corporations who were attracted to fascism along the lines of the French Croix de Feu, attempted to obtain the cooperation of a highly decorated U.S. Marine General named Smedley Darlington Butler, to help them in removing Roosevelt from office.[210] But instead of allowing these

---

[208]Moorehead, Caroline. *Gellhorn: A Twentieth-Century Life,* (New York: Henry Holt, 2003), p. 76.
[209]Ibid, pp. 76-80.
[210]Bakan, Joel. *The Corporation: The Pathological Pursuit Of Profit And Power,* (New York: Free Press, c 2004), pp. 86-94.

financiers to use him as they had done in the past, the general nipped fascism in the bud by exposing their sinister plot.

If he had cooperated with these money barons, who knows what would have happened to our country and to Europe? His refusal to cooperate with these financiers also meant Americans could go on to help stop Hitler in Europe. How close this country came to the dark scenario of fascist rule is chilling. Again, we often can see how the decision of just one individual has the power to change the fate of millions.

There is a lesson here. When compromised governments and wealthy interests collude in secret, freedom and democracy take a hit. The only way to keep people honest is to have enough courage to speak out.

Vulture Funds

A Vulture feeds on death. It waits patiently for it. Vulture Fund bond speculators do the same as they buy up Third-World debts for a very cheap price. They then use bribery and law suits to squeeze multiples of that amount from those same debtor countries. The result is that no actual debt relief happens and all hope is lost for feeding and educating their populations. Argentina has felt the sting of vulture fund strategies.

Hedge funds like NML Capital have taken advantage of Argentina's attempt to pay off its debt in a just and fair resolution. Even the international community is agreeing with Argentina's unwillingness to pay billions of dollars more to vulture hedge-fund creditors.[211]

According to Greg Palast, investigative reporter for the BBC, one of these vulture funds, Donegal International, owned by Michael Sheehan, aimed for $40 million of our tax money earmarked for Aids in Zambia.

When Representatives John Conyers, D (MI) and Donald Payne D (NJ) heard about this, they were so angry they marched into the White House and demanded

---

[211] Lopez, Linette. 2015. Ha! You Thought Argentina Would Negotiate. 8, January. Available @ businessinsider.com

that President Bush close the legal loopholes that allow Vulture funds to feed on dying economies.[212]

The Bush administration could have stopped it with just the stroke of a pen. However, Vulture bond speculators had been one of the administration's major donors. Perhaps the president needed to see the Pulitzer Prize photo showing a vulture sitting on the ground just a few feet away from a bent-over emaciated toddler as it watched that child go through its death thralls.[213] And now, in 2015, the world watches, as Greece weakens even more as a victim of Vulture Funds.[214]

The Dark Shadow Of Racism

In a democratic and free society, no one should have to fear abuse from the very people who are supposed to protect them. But as of yet, despite the passing of the Civil Rights Act, democracy has not automatically guaranteed freedom and safety for everyone. As a result of the increasing black outrage at unrestrained targeting and police violence in many American cities, protest groups have formed to demand justice. In Cleveland, Ohio, over a thousand Black Lives Matter supporters converged for a historic conference to bring attention to this behavior which threatens their very existence.[215] Family members of more than 20 African Americans killed by police spoke out.

Their message was loud and clear—until everyone is free from fear and abuse, no one is free.

Offers We Can't Refuse?

Take the Medicare prescription drug benefit to seniors. In *The Buying of the President,* author Charles Lewis notes that the motivation was really to first benefit the pharmaceutical industry. PhRMA's cozy relationship with government is a well-known fact. As one of the leading influencers in Washington, it has spent

---

[212]Palast, Greg. 2007. *Free Speech TV "Democracy Now, The War and Peace Report"*, discussion with Greg Palast, Investigative Reporter for the BBC. 15 February. Available @ democracynow.org.
[213]Rare Historical Photos. The vulture and the little girl.
[214]nytimes.com/2012/05/16/business/global/bet-on-greek...
[215].cleveland.com/metro/index.ssf/2015/07/thousands_of_freedom_fighters.html

over $1 billion in the ten years between 1994 and 2004.[216] Apparently generic drug competition and all those trips to Canada to buy cheaper drugs were taking a toll on PhRMA's profits. With $150 million spent at the state, federal, and international level—it didn't take long to get a positive response! In just a matter of weeks the bill was passed.[217]

So, who really benefited from this? The thing to be aware of here is how deftly Medicare was being taken out of the hands of the public sector and slowly given over to the private pharmaceutical industry.

Now that President Obama's Health Care Reform Act has reigned in some of the worst abuses of for-profit health insurers, the industry will do everything in its power to continue to preserve itself. But until medical costs are brought down, increasing the availability of health insurance coverage will not be the final solution for the high costs of health care in America.

Social Security reform?

The attempt by the Bush administration to privatize Social Security was troubling. The whole point of Social Security is to protect older Americans as well as disabled Americans from painful manipulations and losses in the stock market as well as financial vulnerability from inflation. The depression of the 1930s was an extremely painful way to learn this lesson.

Now, with advances in health, our populations live longer, making even more critical the security of an economic safety net! The number of seniors living in poverty (3.5 million) doubles (6.5 million) when they are met with medical costs for home health aides, assisted living, and nursing home costs.[218] Granted, there are wealthy Americans for whom social security represents a very small portion of their wealth. But for the majority of Americans, social security is just that—

[216]Lewis, Charles. *The Buying of the President: Who's Really Bankrolling Bush And His Democratic Challengers—And What They Expect in Return*, (New York: Perennial, c2004), p. 105.
[217]Ibid, p. 151.
[218]Poo, Al-Jen and Conrad, Ariane. *The Age Of Dignity*, (New York: The New Press, 2015). P. 33. AARP, press release, December 18, 2012.

social security! And what makes seniors and the disabled more secure also makes their families more secure.

According to the AARP (American Association of Retired Persons) "social security is the *main* source of income for almost two-thirds of older American households and the *sole* source of income for one-third."[219]

Fortunately, the Bush administration's recent attempt to "personalize" Social Security earnings failed. Thank goodness, because, the stock market is particularly vulnerable to the volatility of high frequency trading and unregulated massive speculation. Or as Naomi Klein defines it, "the electronic herd".[220]

Millions lost their retirement nest eggs in the 2008 financial crisis. Older Americans, whose very quality of life depends on their guaranteed social security income, became very close to becoming the next corporate "externalities".

And Social Security is not going broke.

As of July 4. 2014, social Security has a $2.7 trillion surplus and can pay out every benefit owed to every eligible person for the next 19 years. After that, even if we do nothing, it will pay out 85% of benefits owed for the next 75 years.[221]

Social Security has not contributed one penny to the deficit because it is independently funded by the FICA payroll tax.

Kickbacks and Dark Pools

Instead of putting the well-being of our older Americans into the hands of Wall Street speculators, Congress could be addressing their harmful and hidden programs.

In *Flash Boys,* author Michael Lewis describes one of those hidden programs. He writes "Replacing people with machines enabled the markets to become not just faster but more complicated…an incredibly complicated system of fees and kickbacks,"[222] placing the majority of investors at risk.

[219] Ibid.
[220] Klein, Naomi. *The Shock Doctrine: The Rise of Disaster Capitalism,* (New York: Metropolitan Books: Henry Holt, 2007).
[221] socialsecurityworks.org
[222] Lewis, Michael. *Flash Boys: A Wall Street Revolt,* (New York:` W.W. Norton & Company, 2014). p. 35.

And he notes how in 2005 when the exchanges went from being utilities owned by their members to corporations run for profit, the exchanges no longer had a human being handling orders but were replaced by big banks' encoded trading rules (algorithms).[223]

In *Saving Capitalism For the Many, Not the Few,* Robert Reich explains how insider trading, buybacks, and stock options for CEOs and their corporate managers, distort the value of the market.[224] But because these actions are not transparent, the average investor has no way to judge the true value of market shares. These powerful interests actually control the rules by which the exchanges operate, so huge and hidden windfalls can be instantly made, and safely tucked away into the personal accounts of these Wall St. players. Meanwhile, no one is looking out for the average investor.

Instant Wealth vs. Wise Long-Term Investing

At a time when every trick in the book is employed by wealthy and powerful interests who have no concern over the real long-term value of their investments, nor of the effects their actions have on society at large, it is encouraging to see a wiser development in the world of investing.

Generation Investment Management, a healthier approach to investing, concentrates on financial and business activities that are contrary to today's global marketplace. Pioneered by Al Gore and senior partner, David Blood, the goal is *sustainable capitalism*, meaning that environmental and social results of corporate activity are more important than instant short-term gains with their "booms and busts, widening gaps between rich and poor, and the intensifying pressures on the natural environment".[225] Gore "hopes Generation's record will call attention to the message that "the world's investors can't ignore: They can *make more money* if they change their practices in a way that will, at the same time, also reduce the environmental and social damage modern capitalism can do.

---

[223]Ibid.
[224]Reich, Robert B. *Saving Capitalism For the Many, Not the Few.* (New York Alred A. Knopf, 2015).
[225]Fallows, James. 2015. The Investment Secrets of Al Gore. *The Atlantic.* November.

Deregulation As a Business Strategy

Deregulation is a very effective corporate business strategy. Fossil fuel and mining operations get a pass on safety and environmental issues. Pharmaceutical companies get a pass on drug safety and costs. Nuclear plants get a pass on safe operating regulations…the list goes on and on. Meanwhile, for every regulation that is weakened, human beings and the environment are left holding the bag.

Again, this is another example of how weakening and eliminating regulatory agencies removes vital protections for the majority of citizens.

Mining is another good example. The Mine Safety and Health Administration (MSHA) is the watchdog of mine safety. Unfortunately, since it has been one of the more recent victims of anti-regulation policy, effective safety officers, fines, and tough safety laws have been ignored.

The January 2006 disasters at the Sago mine in West Virginia in which 12 miners died, and the Aracoma Coal Co. mine in Logan County in which 2 miners died, are the direct results of this failure of regulation.[226] Had effective safety measurements been put in place, these miners would still be alive today. But if the choice was between a miner's safety and mining industry profits, miners' safety got ignored.

Buying Up Congress

Millions of dollars are donated yearly to Democrats and Republicans by Wall St., electric utilities, telephone companies, credit card companies, chemical companies, pharmaceutical industries, mining companies, health insurance companies, oil interests, and defense manufacturers.

Because average Americans do not have that kind of money, rules of the economic game are skewed to favor the wealthy. Unfortunately, if your desire is to serve, and you run for national office, you must raise millions of dollars. That means you must constantly focus on where and how donations will stream in. And what do these corporations expect for their generosity?

---

[226]Reece, Erik. 2006. Who Killed The West Virginia Miners? *The Nation*. 9 February.

The pharmaceutical industry can count on the law to make it illegal to buy many cheaper over the counter drugs available in other countries instead of their prescription drugs here in the United States and it can prevent the U.S. government from bargaining for lower costs, thereby depriving needy patients who can no longer afford their drugs. Also courts can allow the patenting of the manufacturing processes on vaccines and products derived from nature (which before the 1990s was forbidden).[227] Regarding big pharma, Robert Reich writes that "In 2013, their lobbying tab came to $225 million, which was more than the lobbying expenditures of America's military contractors."[228]

The health insurance industry can amass huge wealth while ignoring the reality of helpless un-insured Americans.[229]

Internet and Cable companies can merge into more powerful anti-competitive positions, raise our rates, and decrease our choices, while also giving us the slowest speeds among advanced nations. The revolving door is active in Washington for the cable companies. Reich writes: "Michael Powell, who chaired the Federal Communications Commission (FCC) in 2002, subsequently became head of the cable industry's lobbying group. The National Cable and Telecommunications Association ranked twelfth in lobbyist spending in 2014.)"[230]

Chemical, oil, mining, and manufacturing industries can get our tax money while dumping their wastes wherever it is convenient. Private media can consolidate to control our news and make immense profits by the great wealth poured into electoral campaigns. Banks that find themselves in crisis for defrauding the public can avoid footing the bill or going to jail for their criminal behavior. Meanwhile, we citizens foot the bill to the tune of billions of dollars.

---

[227]Reich, Robert B. *Saving Capitalism For the Many, Not the Few.* (New York: Alfred A. Knopf, 2015). pp. 23, 24.

[228]Ibid., p.25.

[229] Potter, Wendell. *Deadly spin: an insurance company insider speaks out on how corporate PR is killing health care and deceiving Americans.* (New York: Bloomsbury Press, 2010).

[230]Reich, Robert B. *Saving Capitalism For the Many, Not the Few.*(New York: Alfred A. Knopf, 2015). pp.31, 33.

Elections

Direct elections were never a political reality in America; in the 2000 election, Al Gore won the popular election with 50,999,897 votes (half a million more than George Bush).[231]

Much criticism has been focused on our Electoral College but as Arthur Schlesinger, Jr. in his book *War And The American Presidency* points out, "direct elections would not only encourage splinter candidates in many single issues, but would drain votes, and produce many run-off elections with corrupt bargains for pledges of support."[232]

To prevent the popular vote loser from becoming the electoral vote winner, Schlesinger suggested that a national bonus plan could be adopted. It would award the popular-vote winner a bonus of two electoral votes for each state and the District of Columbia, thus reserving "both the constitutional and practical role of the states in presidential elections".[233]

Machines and Restrictive Voting Laws

Issues like hanging chads and election fraud, have caused many districts in the country to be supplied with electronic voting machines. The only problem was that there was no way to produce hard backup copies and the machines were open to abuse and manipulation. To make matters worse, recently passed laws adding new restrictions on voting, placed a new and unnecessary burden on citizens— many of whom had already been voting for years.

One of those efforts to disenfranchise students, the elderly, racial minorities, and the poor, took the form of requiring photo ID's to prove one's identity. Apparently, social security cards were not enough.

There was also a $250 fine for each registration turned in 10 days after it was signed.[234] This promised to do away with another several thousand votes from

[231]Remnick, David. *REPORTING: Writings From The New Yorker.* (New York: Knopf, 2006). p. 4.
[232]Schlesinger, Jr., Arthur. *War And The American Presidency.* (W.W. Norton & Company, New York: 2004), P. 103.
[233]Ibid.
[234]2006. *WGBH, PBS NOW with David Brancacchio,* Voting Restrictions: Putting Up Barriers in the Name of Stopping Voter Fraud. 1 September.

people who may have been late turning in their forms due to a natural or family emergency.

Voters have been taken off voting lists because they simply have a name that is suspect or that can be tweaked, or they are accused of having had a criminal history, or because they simply are easily identified as belonging to the wrong ethnic group.

In Oregon more than 4,600 voters had their ballots rejected based on a signature mismatch.[235] Interesting that matching signatures are not required by Oregon law—they must only be verified by the voter.

In a democracy, voting is a right; it is not a luxury reserved for the privileged and the wealthy. In a democracy all our votes count and the process of voting should be made easy and convenient.

Never Judge a Bill by its Title

What has homeland security got to do with off-shore tax evasion?

The answer is nothing. In *The Buying of the President,* Charles Lewis tells us that in 2002 after Democrats were successful in preventing the awarding of lucrative government contracts to tax-dodging corporations like Tyco, Ingersoll-Rand, and Accenture, Republicans reversed it:

> "…the Republican leadership, in consultation with the White House, abruptly introduced a revised homeland Security bill that effectively gutted the offshore-contracting prohibition ….What's more, Republicans sidestepped committees and quietly buried a number of other eleventh-hour provisions in the 500-page bill."[236]

Lewis points out how secret deals that sneak in last minute provisions and tax breaks for privileged interests are hidden in bills that are so thick, it is nearly impossible to catch them. And they are often furtively put through on holiday weekends when no one is available to see it. This practice has claimed billions of our tax dollars. It's great strategy for higher corporate profits, but for working-

---

[235] Oregon Right To Know. 12/12/14.
[236] Charles Lewis. *The Buying of the President: Who's Really Bankrolling Bush And His Democratic Challengers—And What They Expect in Return,* (New York: Perennial c2004), pp. 207, 208.

class citizens it means bearing the financial burden of government while losing its protections. The average American citizen is not only unaware of these shenanigans but what is even worse, has little voice with which to prevent them.

Who Influences Our Democracy?

If it is a choice between millions of sick people in need of medical attention who cannot afford health insurance or a corporate lobbyist with a large donation, who do you think gets the ears of many elected officials?

In a choice between ending the War in Iraq, which is what most Americans wanted, or continuing to finance it, which was what Wall St., Halliburton, Bechtel, Blackwater, and Lockheed Martin wanted, we could have put our money on "staying the course".

When we are warned of the toxicity of nuclear energy and the danger of nuclear weapons, how likely is it that the military and energy production will no longer engage in nuclear solutions?

When the majority of the world's population would put an end to more fossil fuel development, how likely is it that we will leave it in the ground?

When more and more people are suspicious of the produce in their supermarkets, what are the chances that GMO labeling will appear on those shelves?

When college students are drowning in debt, how soon will bills be introduced in Congress to lower the high cost of private college debt and succeed?

When more and more Americans become victims of gun violence how likely is it that effective gun control laws will pass?

After all, the first goal of a for-profit enterprise is to maximize its shareholder wealth—not maximize a healthy planet or the quality of life for all its citizens.

Exporting Democracy

Apparently, our system of democracy in which private interests are paramount, is the envy of all and our military and free trade economic policies are God's tools to spread it to the rest of the world.

Yet, not everyone is convinced that privatizing essential infrastructure is a desirable move toward democracy. Instead of democratization, most people see it as theft and exploitation of their natural resources. In *An Ordinary Person's Guide To Empire,* author Arundhati Roy writes:

> "All over the world today, freedoms are being curbed in the name of protecting freedom. Once freedoms are surrendered by civil society, they cannot be retrieved without a struggle. ...Empire is on the move, and Democracy is its sly new war cry."[237]

She notes how forcing farmers to re-invest yearly in Monsanto's genetically modified seeds instead of using their own, as well as dam building required by the World Trade Organization, has done great harm to more than thirty-three million people.[238] Referring to a report of the World Commission on Dams, Roy notes that an average rural family in India is worse off than it was before the dams.[239] In addition, the move to hastily build factories is another problem. It not only wipes out the livelihoods of indigenous workers and fishing communities but also pollutes their ecosystem.[240]

This much praised free-trade economy has taken away government subsidies, as well as previously protected farm credits and produce outlets from farmers. Once those protections are removed, hunger, prostitution, trafficking, and violence soon develop.

These have been on the increase in rural communities of India. In Alexander Cockburn's 2006 article in *The Nation,* he writes about the increase of women on India's highways, waiting for pickups by truck drivers over the past twelve years."[241] And at the World Economic Forum in Davos in 1999 at which all the world's wealthy met, Guatemala's foreign minister announced, "Destruction carries with it an opportunity for foreign investment."[242]

---

[237]Roy, Arundhati. *Guide to Empire* (Cambridge, Massachusetts: South End Press c2004), pp. 17, 47.
[238]Ibid, p. 14.
[239]Ibid, pp. 102, 103.
[240]Ibid, p. 19
[241]Cockburn, Alexander. 2006. Nick Kristof's Brothel Problem. *The Nation.*
13 February.
[242]Klein, Naomi. *The Shock Doctrine: The Rise of Disaster Capitalism,* (New York: Metropolitan Books/ 2007), p. 396.

One of those opportunities was taken by Telmex, Mexico's privatized phone company. By buying up Guatemala's telecom system, Telmex made an offer that Guatemala couldn't refuse.[243]

To see how these opportunities are played out by the Central America Free Trade Agreement (CAFTA) one has only to look at their non-existent child-labor policies.

For example, in food processing, temperatures must always be kept very low. So, wearing only sneakers, children's' feet are often in cold water as the vegetables they process are washed. Activist and executive director of the National Labor Committee, Charles Kernaghan notes that the Legumex food processing factory in Guatemala has employed children as young as thirteen in 12-hour shifts..[244]

In South America, countries like Ecuador and Colombia, have also been ravaged by the construction of big dams and oil discoveries.[245] But many countries are now speaking out and refusing to lose their sovereignty to large corporations.

In Bolivia, the move has begun toward independence from the World Bank and the IMF. Bolivians want a more authentic democracy. They've made protection of the rights of indigenous communities their priority. In August of 2006, their Constitutional Assembly put through reforms to nationalize their mines, distribute lands and sign new contracts with natural gas companies.[246]

Venezuela has done the same.

In Hawaii, Hawaiian Indigenous Activist, Mililani Trask, notes that globalization's exploitation of Pacific Island Nation States' natural resources has threatened the most diverse marine environment in the world. Hawaii has the

---

[243]Ibid.
[244]2007. Guatemala child labor under CAFTA. *Free Speech TV, "Democracy Now, The War and Peace Report"*. 13 March. Available @ democracynow.org.
[245]Perkins, John. *Confessions of an Economic Hit Man*, (San Francisco CA: Berrett-Koehler, c2004), pp. xviii, xix.
[246]Villca, Felex. 2006. Indigenous Peoples' Resistance to Economic Globalization: A Celebration of Victories, Rights, and Cultures. International Forum On Globalization. 23 November Available @ democracynow.org

world's largest number of trans-national corporations working on genetic modification activities in the Pacific.[247]

In the November, 2014 ballot initiatives to require GMO labeling, Hawaii's Maui County (often referred to as GMO Ground Zero) was a unique success story. It successfully passed one of the strongest anti-GMO measures in spite of the fact that Monsanto outspent it by a ratio of 87 to 1. But predictively, in order to prevent enforcement, Monsanto plans to ask the Maui court to declare this initiative "legally flawed."[248] (And if the TPP trade agreement had been in effect, Monsanto could have sued the government for the reduction in Monsanto's anticipated future profits that this anti-GMO measure had caused, thereby further weakening the tax base!)

Profits vs People

In commenting on empirical activities in the Arab world, Andrew Bacevich, West Point Graduate, Vietnam veteran, and professor of history and international relations at Boston University pointed out:

> "...those activities, have never been motivated by British concern, French concern, or American concern, about the well-being of the people who live there. That presence has been motivated by imperial ambition, by desire to have access to oil, by geopolitical calculations relative to the Soviet Union back in the Cold War days."[249]

Serving Two Masters

Lauding the virtues of democracy, while at the same time supporting free markets abroad, which are eroding democracy, gets our government into trouble. In trying to hold on to its dual identity—a champion of democracy, while at the same time, its opposite, an enabler of free trade— the United States has come across as hypocritical. But there is always that pesky middle-class to deal with.

---

[247]Ibid.
[248]2014. Maui v. Monsanto: Hawaii County Voters Defy Agri-Giant's Spending to OK Landmark Ban on GMO Crops. *Free Speech TV, "Democracy Now-The War and Peace Report".* 6 November. Available @ democracynow.org
[249]Bacevich, Andrew. 2012. Interview with Andrew Bacevich. *Moyers and Company.* 23 March. Available @ billmoyers.com.

A middle-class encourages democracy, and whenever it is created, what follows is always a birth of democratic ideas. For example, in Spain, an exemplary citizen movement has succeeded in forcing banks to negotiate. Ada Colau, a longtime anti-eviction activist, has become Barcelona's first female mayor.[250]

She explains that Spain's economic crisis is a consequence of a profound democratic crisis where the cozy relationship between political elites and economic elites has ruined the economy, with the banks as the ultimate defrauder.

Inequality has shot up causing social setbacks in health and education, leading to broken families, diseases, and suicide. She says that all over Europe citizens' city councils are confronting financial elites declaring that they want governments that serve its citizens—not the private interests.[251]

2015. *Free Speech TV "Democracy Now, The War and Peace Report"*, discussion with Ada Colau, Mayor of Barcelona, Spain. 5 June. Available @ democracynow.org.
[250]Ibid.
[251]Ibid.

CHAPTER FIVE   THE WORLD OF SCIENCE

"The first child whose genes come at least in part from some corporate lab, the first child who has been "enhanced" from what came before—that's the first child who will glance back over his shoulder and see a gap between himself and human history."[252]

- Bill McKibben, *Enough*

This new world is coming and it is coming fast. Along with the environment, the human being of the twenty-first century is now the latest fertile ground for scientific tinkering.

Developments will not only involve more space exploration, physics, cosmology, nanotechnology, and stem-cell research, but also synthetic biology, germline engineering, drones, robotics, and discoveries we probably couldn't even guess at.

With each new breakthrough the benefits promised will be great, but so will the dangers. Not enough that plants and animals are increasingly under the control of transnational corporations—we now have transgenic animals and genetically modified crops.[253]

The next horizon will be to break the taboo on human genetic modification. In his book, *Enough,* Bill McKibben makes the distinction between somatic gene therapy and germline genetic engineering:

> "Somatic gene therapy, which aims at specific diseases and attempts to neutralize them, is like medicine and it holds great promise. On the other hand,

---

Chapter Five   The World of Science

[252]McKibben, Bill. En*ough: Staying Human In An Engineered Age,* (New York: Times Books, c2003.), p. 65.
[253]Glavin, Terry. *The Sixth Extinction: journey among the lost and left behind.* (New York: Thomas Dunne Books/St. Martin's Press, 2007).

germline genetic engineering is taking us down a different road. It involves the artificially changing of our bodies with pre-designed genes in order to genetically engineer a new human. In other words, this science is completely redesigning our healthy cells. He warns that this research is being aided by lower and lower costs, making it very problematic.[254]

He quotes the clinician, Gina Kolata:

"...biotechnology is forging way ahead of biology, ethics, and common sense. All of us think about this all the time. All of the clinicians wonder what we are doing."[255]

The danger in research by for-profit commercial interests is that the safety and welfare of the public never comes first. This is seen over and over again as our environment and human health have suffered abuse and destruction at the hands of those whose only goal is greater profits.

My Child Is Perfect

Some engineers in the corporate world are already planning for the day when they can design our future children. They are counting on the fact that parents of the future will not want to deny their children these advantages. Thus, we could no longer be a human *being* but a human *product* to satisfy a consumer-driven society.

And why not? Corporations have already successfully re-defined themselves as holding "people" status, so what's to stop them from re-defining people into "product" status? We could genetically create superior groups, as opposed to inferior groups. But keep in mind, just as with any consumer product; we could see the day when purchasing one or more designer genes for your baby won't be much different from buying any other consumer product. Buyers' remorse could apply if the genetic program you select for your baby disappoints. Lest we forget, all this will be driven by the profit motive and the concept known as "planned obsolescence".

---

[254]McKibben, Bill. En*ough: Staying Human In An Engineered Age*, (New York: Times Books, c2003. p. 17.
[255]Ibid.

In a few years, your child would be certain to become obsolete. In this brave new world you could see commercials comparing the comparative benefits of newer corporate engineered babies over the older versions. Updating your child would be a new market to be exploited.

We may think our society is polarized and unequal today, but as McKibben points out, in a world of artificially designed humans we could actually breed a caste system.[256] In *The Sixth Extinction,* author Terry Glavin goes even further. Commenting on the possibility of genetically-altered humans, he refers to them as "parahumans" and "humanzees"[257] with no human rights and ordered to do our work. And here we thought we were finally rid of the evil of slavery!

The True Brain of the Cell

Bruce Lipton, author of *The Biology of Belief,* [258] points out that genes are not the only controller of our biology after all; new research shows that the environment the genes live in is much more strategic than the genes themselves. He says it is the cell membrane, (not the gene) that controls our behavior and if the membrane dies, the cell dies too. Because the cell membrane, independent of the genes, actually decides what it will allow to pass through it and what it will ignore; it acts in the same way as does a silicon chip in a computer.[259]

Like a computer, Lipton notes that our cells are programmable and like the computer, the programmer is not inside the cell, but outside of it.[260] But what Lipton found really amazing is that not only do receptor proteins respond to physical signals, they also read vibrational energy (non-physical signals). [261] This questions the belief that only physical molecules are involved in cell physiology.

This new information is significant for us at this critical point in our evolution. Evolution can be seen as the history of cells banding together in cooperation, to

---

[256]Ibid, p. 38.
[257]Glavin, Terry. *The Sixth Extinction,* (New York: Thomas Dunne Books/St.l Martin's Press, 2007), p. 29.
[258]Lipton, Bruce. *The Biology Of Belief,* (Santa Rosa, CA: Mountain of Love/Elite Books, c 2005. pp. 76-84.
[259]Ibid, p. 91.
[260]Ibid.
[261]Ibid, p. 88

share their awareness. And now human beings are challenged to band together in increased awareness. And through our ability to control what information is allowed into our brain cells, we are the drivers of our own evolution.

Nanotechnology

Nanomaterial is material that consists of nano-sized (extremely small) particles. (one nanometer is one-millionth the length of a grain of sand).[262] Nanoparticles less than 300 nm are so small they pass through biological membranes and enter cells. They have physical, chemical, and biological properties that are different from larger particles of the same molecules—thus, making them more biologically active.[263] Silver nanoparticles have been found to cause cell death in humans as well as in mice testicular cells, and some types of both titanium dioxide and zinc oxide nanoparticles are toxic to human brain and lung cells.[264]

In spite of the fact that research on the potential risk from these nanoparticles has been lacking, this technology has taken off in the food industry. "The Food and Drug Administration has recognized that ingredients that are generally recognized as safe at the macro level may not be safe at the nanoscale."[265] And this introduction of nanotechnology into the food industry has initiated concern not only for consumers, but also for shareholders.

Because of the potential dangers of titanium dioxide being used as a whitening agent, the non-profit organization, As You Sow, a tax-exempt 501(c)3 non-profit organization which has as its vision a safe, just, and sustainable world in which protecting the environment and human rights is central to corporate decision making, successfully commissioned independent laboratory testing of Dunkin' Donuts' white powdered donuts.

As a result of this testing, Dunkin' Donuts announced that they no longer use the titanium dioxide whitening agent.[266]

---

[262]asyousow.org/our-work/environmental-health/nanomaterials/
[263]Ibid.
[264]Ibid.
[265]Ibid.
[266]Ibid.

Nanobots

James Martin notes that in the future, millions of nanobots will be able to be introduced directly into our brain via the blood stream. He writes:

> "Through wireless technology, these nanobots will communicate with software on the internet and interact with our neurons. It will be possible to live in a world of brain enhancement in which parents will be encouraged to buy brain transponder enhancement kits for their children.[267] Some have even promoted uploading the brain into a computer, thus, we could have silicon humans."[268]

To pay allegiance to the current belief that genetic tinkering will remove all our imperfections is a sure recipe for disaster. Yet, genetically modified crops are only the beginning. There is now the designing and engineering of a new future human being. Futurist, author, and inventor, Raymond Kurzweil, predicts that because humans are linear by nature and technology is exponential, artificial intelligence will supplant human intelligence as the most capable processing power.[269]

An even more bizarre development is seen in the field of robotics. Kurzweil believes that "People willing to give up their 'wet bodies'—we're 50% to 60% water—could not only live forever but also think at electronic speeds."[270]

Martin warns that more new buzzwords like "Transhumanism" will be in our future.[271]

But humans are not computers. He points out that a human being is unique, can dream, can have common sense, and a wide expanse of experience while computers will have infinite depth only. The two will never be equal.[272]

Where is the Mind?

For those who would credit the brain for the source of intelligence Schroeder reminds us that nowhere in the brain can the mind be found. Yet we are always

---

[267]Martin, James. *The Meaning of the 21st Century*, (New York: 2006), pp. 347-349.
[268]Ibid, p. 352.
[269]http://en.wikipedia.org/wiki/Ray_Kurzweil#Future_predictions
[270]2005. *Business Week*. Raymond C. Kurzweil, "Voices of Innovation: Prophet of Longevity". 1 August.
[271]Martin, James. *The Meaning of the 21st Century*, (New York: 2006), P. 198.
[272]Ibid, pp. 191-192.

conscious of ourselves, even in our dreams.[273] In *The Gentle Art of Spiritual Guidance,* John Yungblut quotes the paleontologist, Teilhard de Chardin: "Spirit sprang from the womb of matter...matter is the only chalice that can hold the wine of spirit."[274] Like gravity, spirit is invisible. It cannot be measured in a lab. The unity of body, mind, and spirit is not a divided concept.

Mind is everywhere in nature as we observe it in plants, animals, fish and birds. Mind has always been there; it didn't just begin with us. We live in a unified and interconnected universe that generates and uses information. This same connecting intelligence is also in every one of our cells. Without this consciousness, our bodies would not be the marvels they are.

The thing to keep in mind is that in evolution, the biological, psychological and spiritual work together as a whole. In a conversation exploring the relationships between humans, technology, and culture, Intel Futurist, Brian Johnson, along with Director of Jewish Studies, Dr. Hava Tirosh-Samuelson, discussed the dangers inherent in this futuristic movement. She explains that not everything can be digitized:

> "You cannot engineer love, responsibility, caring...we do not need
> a perfectionistic future...we need to humanize our future...we need a
> world with deeper culture."[275]

Just as we can never be reduced to the simple chemicals from which we are made, just as the great works of art can never be reduced to their pigments, just as great literature and poetry can never be reduced to just letters of the alphabet, and just as inspiring music can never be reduced to just notes on a musical scale, we can never be reduced to bits and bytes. This is an example of left-brain technology without the balance of right-brain wisdom.

---

[273]Schroeder, Gerald. *The Hidden Face of God: How Science Reveals The Ultimate Truth,* (New York: 2001), p. 147.

[274]Yungblut, John R., *The Gentle Art of Spiritual Guidance*, (New York: Amity House, Inc. 1988), p. 44.

[275]Tirosh-Samuelson, Dr. Hava and Johnson, Brian. 2013. Transhumanism. "Exploring Relationships Between Humans, Technology, and Culture". Conversation between Dr. Hava Tirosh-Samuelson and Brian Johnson.14 January. Available @ future.wikia.com.

Anything that would lead us away from our bodies is leading us away from our wholeness. Putting our scientists up on a pedestal is just as worrisome as minimizing their great contributions to humanity. Computers will never be human and humans will never be computers. We can never continue to evolve through technology alone, while leaving our human spirit behind. Neither are human beings products to be marketed.

We are human beings with a divine destiny and a divine right to be left alone. Each of us is unique—regardless of our status or station in life. The conscious intelligence in our cells must not be replaced by a left-brained corporate synthetic intelligence produced and manipulated by a chip. We have gone from citizens to consumers and now we're on the way to synthetic immortality!

Should we be so foolish as to allow our healthy cells to be replaced with alien cells or be artificially enhanced with chips, we may have everything to lose—our souls, our privacy, our very humanity. And, just in case, we think common sense would never let things get that far, McKibben notes that in a 1995 study, almost 100 Olympic hopefuls were willing to take a fatal drug if they thought it would give them a five-year winning streak.[276]

Computer as Ally—Not Replacement

When Deep Blue, IBM's RS 6000 SP computer took on the world chess champion Gary Kasparov in 1997 and won, a sense of anxiety began about the computer's potential to surpass our human brain.[277] This scenario repeats as the computerized Watson competes with humans in the game of Jeopardy. However, Deep Blue and Watson were programmed by man.

Jennifer Cobb, in her book, *Cybergrace,* gives us her vision of the great potential of cooperation between man and machine. She points out how we are beginning

---

[276]McKibben, Bill. *Enough: Staying Human In An Engineered Age,* (New York: Times Books, c2003), p. 4.
[277]Cobb, Jennifer J. *Cybergrace: The Search For God In A Digital World,* (New York: Crown, c1998), pp. 1-5.

to see that as humanity advances in its complexity, the old clear distinctions begin to blur.[278]

She explains that no longer can the universe be divided into tidy separate categories of mind and matter; today science knows better. Our minds and our bodies are not separate, but operate as one. In other words we are connected to consciousness—we are consciousness.[279]

As we know, when we surf the Web, we go off in any direction depending on the relationships we're after. Like quantum physics, the experience is completely open and unpredictable. Just as in real life, the internet is integrative and connected; there are no walls of separation.

Cyberspace simply mirrors the holographic conscious intelligence network which pervades the universe and to which we are all connected. We are the latest fruits of this universal intelligence. Cobb tells us that cyberspace can help us to further our spiritual and planetary evolution. But she also warns that we have created computers; they will be our allies, but never our replacements![280]

Everything Is Connected

In fact, all scientific disciplines are pointing to the fact that seeing our world as made up of separate objects is a mistaken illusion.

In *Science And The Akashic Field*, author Ervin Laszlo tells us that space is not a vacuum. Instead, we live in a meaningful and informed social universe.

> "... particles and atoms are not individual beasts. They are sociable entities ... in all pertinent places at the same time. Their nonlocality respects neither time nor space; it exists whether the distance that separates the particles and the atoms is measured in millimeters or in light-years, and whether the time that separates them consists of seconds or of millions of years."[281]

In *Creation How Science Is Reinventing Life* Itself, author Adam Rutherford writes:

---

[278]Ibid, p. 7.
[279]Ibid, p. 105.
[280]Ibid.
[281]Laszlo, Ervin. *Science and the Akashic Field: An Integral Theory of Everything,* (Rochester, VT.: Inner Traditions, 2004), pp. 33, 34.

"I believe that scientific research should occur in the full glare of public scrutiny and that scientists should engage with publics of all levels of expertise. This way, with data out in the open, and informed public conversations about the potential benefit and the potential harm that new technologies create, we foster a society in which rational approaches to global and local problems are normalized...[282]

Here again, we might consider some very important questions. How free will we be to refuse to have these modifications forced upon us? How much of this research is without any supervision, transparency, or control? Do we appreciate the ethical significance of these activities? And finally, should ordinary citizens even care? These questions become very important when our human destiny is on the line.

Has any corporate engineer created the billions of stars in the Milky Way, a sun, a planet, or a prokaryote? All of these have evolved without our tinkering. We are wisdom's latest achievements. Do we really want to break that link?

As we know, left brain and right brain form a symbiotic relationship. Humanity needs the whole of our intelligence, including our right-brain intuition and wisdom. One without the other sends us off course into precarious realms. There is a destiny for humanity and it will take more than profit-driven left-brained corporate technology to achieve it.

Given that Olympic athletes were willing to die to win a medal, it's quite possible that there would be human beings willing to be uploaded into a robot to live forever. That certainly would be dramatic! But as McKibben points out, human cloning, germ line engineering and a downloaded brain do not answer the question, who am I?

---

[282]Rutherford, Adam. *Creation How Science Is Reinventing Life Itself.* (New York: Penguin Group 2013) pp. 194, 231.

CHAPTER SIX   OUR INTERNATIONAL SYSTEM

"In Rwanda the massacre of around 800,000 Tutsis by Hutu [gangs] in April-July 1994 took place after international efforts to democratize the regime"[283]

- Michael Hirsh, *At War With Ourselves*

The United Nations Vision

When we think of international politics, the United Nations comes to mind. Initially, it was believed that a peaceful world could be brought about by this body. But it didn't take long to learn that the UN is simply a mirror of the world at large, and as such it has built-in divisions and opposing ideologies, making it impossible to function effectively.

It failed to protect victims of genocide in Rwanda, Somalia, and the Sudan. It failed to prevent the rape of hundreds of thousands of women and young girls in the Congo. It failed to stop ethnic cleansing in Eastern Europe. It failed to prevent the Six-Day War. It failed in the Arab-Israeli conflict, and in the Gaza Strip Israeli attacks. The same is true of the conflicts in Afghanistan and Pakistan. And it has not stopped the human carnage in Syria, Iraq, Yemen and Africa.   However, it certainly isn't inexpensive! Hirsh notes that soon after 2000 the UN's peace-keeping budget had gone up from $600 million to $3 billion per year.[284]

But peace, apparently, cannot be bought.

Chapter Six   Our International System

[283]Hirsh, Michael. *At War With Ourselves: Why America Is Squandering Its Chance To Build A Better World*, (New York: Oxford University Press, 2003), p. 173.
[284]Ibid, P. 193.

Free Trade

To understand the world today, it is necessary to look at how it is being regulated by its major non-government organizations. In *At War With Ourselves,* author Michael Hirsh refers us to The World Trade Organization (WTO), The World Bank (WB), and the International Monetary Fund (IMF). To partake of this global economy, countries must bend to the dictates of the WTO and then to borrow the money to play, they must go to the IMF.[285]

He describes globalization as mainly an economic phenomenon which began when foreign exchange controls were removed allowing for free trade. Up till then the concept of globalism was understood to be the "Cold War system of treaties and international institutions and law"[286] which stabilized the international community.

Globalism can be understood as an evolving democratic ideal. It is a reflection of the international community, with its treaties and laws. Along with its protection of national sovereignty, globalism must deal with the rights of individuals to be equally heard within the family of nations. The United Nations serves this purpose. The unique characteristics of the many different nations are not going away and they shouldn't. They each make an important contribution to the whole. Anything that threatens their existence threatens our evolving human family.

However, coupled with the aid of modern computer technology, removing foreign exchange controls allowed huge sums of private capital to be put to work threatening this global system. In the rush for instant wealth and high shareholder returns, as soon as a country's financial position is threatened, huge sums of shareholder money pull out, leaving the assaulted country in even worse financial condition.

Globalization, according to Naomi Klein, was inspired by the University of Chicago's Milton Friedman. She points out how Milton Friedman's "laissez-

---

[285]Ibid, P. 174.
[286]Ibid. P. 105.

faire" doctrine of free-trade[287] and the elimination of government's public sphere has forced country after country to be sold off to transnational corporations who have grown rich and fat off the backs of each of those victimized countries.

Free Trade Agreements

Russia's present oligarchic economy benefited greatly by IMF money flowing into it after the Cold War. But its people did not as tens of millions of people were stripped of access to their own money.

Klein points out that in one way, the Russians were different from other countries that have fallen victim to disaster economics. Instead of selling off their country to foreigners, the Russians kept it in the hands of their own corrupt local oligarchs, allowing only foreign investment.[288]

Mexico is another good example. By privatizing that country's government services, ordinary citizens became powerless while powerful oligarchs stuffed their pockets. NAFTA allowed foreigners to own Mexican banks thus resulting in those same foreigners getting three times as much government subsidies as that spent on Mexico's own needs.[289]

And with little hope for gainful employment, drug cartels have had no problem enlisting the unemployed as well as police in their illegal activities. Now there is so much violence as a result of Mexico's drug wars that it is almost impossible to curb it.

In demanding justice, Mexico's teachers and citizens' groups have put their lives on the line; they've been beaten, imprisoned, pulled out of their homes, captured, and killed.[290]

The same has been true for other countries in Central America.

---

[287]Klein, Naomi. *The Shock Doctrine: The Rise of Disaster Capitalism*, (New York: Metropolitan Books, Henry Holt, 2007), p. 7.
[288]Ibid., p. 231.
[289]Faux, Jeff. 2006. The Party of Davos. The Nation. 13 February.
[290]2006. Headlines. Mexico Releases 42 Protesters in Oaxaca. *Free Speech TV, "Democracy Now-The War And Peace Report"*. 19 December. Available @ democracynow.org.

Is Free Trade Fair?

Free trade shouldn't leave a country's citizens holding an empty bag. This exercise in "free trade" has allowed an open field for environmental pollution, disregard for education, exploitation of cheap labor, and a disintegration of infrastructure. By pushing through the North American Free Trade Agreement (NAFTA), our own U.S. government has played a role in this new disaster economy.

Free Trade Agreements such as NAFTA and CAFTA, pushed by both Democrats and Republicans, gave international investors a power over the rest of the world that they never should have had. Much like the law which gave corporations the same legal status as a human being, these trade agreements allow huge multi-nationals to steal the rights and government protections from indigenous peoples within their own countries. It's not rocket science to see why people in the countries of Central America and South America would really prefer to carry on without any more meddling from these trade agreements.

According to the Economic Policy Institute, NAFTA promised to add 200,000 jobs to the U.S. economy. But it didn't. As a result, nearly 700,000 jobs were lost. Another 2.7 million jobs were lost due to the Permanent Normal Trade Relations with China, along with the loss of 70,000 jobs as a result of the Korea Free Trade Agreement.[291]

TPP and Fast Track

The Trans-Pacific Partnership (TPP), is the next massive new trade agreement. It is negotiated in secret by 600 corporate advisers along with leaders from twelve Pacific Rim countries representing 40 percent of the global economy. Lori Wallach, director of Public Citizen's Global Trade Watch, refers to this secretive trade deal as a "corporate Trojan horse".[292] And because it is conducted in secrecy

---

[291] Economic Policy Institute. See rootstrikers.org
[292] 2015. Discussion with Rep. Alan Grayson and Lori Wallach, director of Public Citizen's Global Trade Watch. (www.isdscorporateattacks.org) *Free Speech TV, "Democracy Now-The War and Peace Report".16* April. Available @ democracynow.org.

it intentionally keeps the information away from the American people. But thanks to WikiLeaks exposure, some of that information has been leaked to the public.

Wallach notes that the investment chapter of TPP promotes offshoring by giving subsidies to countries who relocate their investments, as well as special privileges and protections that make it cheaper and safe to move jobs to low-wage countries.[293] From what the past has shown us regarding trade agreements and how profits trump people, it is certain that the TPP is not designed to benefit populations or the environment.

And now that "Citizens United" has given corporations the status of a human being, the TPP gives corporations the ability to challenge nations. Called Investor-State Dispute Resolution, the TPP intends to create a tribunal in which corporations can sue governments whose laws interfere with a company's claimed future profits.

So corporations could drag a sovereign government to a tribunal of three private-sector trade attorneys who could also *alternate* as judges. These attorneys could order a government to pay with its tax dollars if they think land zoning, wages, laws governing food safety, access to medicine, intellectual property rights, and environmental protections, violate their new corporate rights.

Wallach notes that out of the agreement's 29 chapters, only five have to do with trade, the others are a sneak attack on governmental democracy. Empowering corporations to directly sue countries, states, counties or cities in order to protect corporations from any legal action that they claim reduces their future profits, will be our undoing.

Corporations could overrule any law and policy that addresses internet freedom, banking and finance regulations, buy-local, food safety ordinances, environmental issues, and living wages, making these laws powerless.[294]

Furthermore, says Wallach, the TPP, would ban the U.S. government from signing any contract with a local domestic Buy America company. If it did, the U.S. would be faced with perpetual trade sanctions and fines from a TPP

---

[293]Ibid.
[294]Ibid.

tribunal.[295] So, by extracting cash from citizens' tax-payer dollars, they would be punished for the crime of undermining TPP's future profits.

Florida Representative Alan Grayson, who along with the majority of democrats in the House of Representatives, opposes Fast Track, saying it will continue the downward trend of the economy, until foreigners own everything. He says the groups that are lobbying the hardest for this are the multinational corporations and their K Street lobbyists. From the beginning, the contents of this agreement have been classified by the administration and trade representatives. Congress and the American people were being denied the information.

As the first member of Congress to actually see any part of the TPP, Representative Grayson was told he couldn't take the information home, couldn't make notes on it, couldn't have his staff present, and didn't want him to discuss it with the media, the public or even other members of Congress.[296]

Citizens in Australia, New Zealand, Peru, Malaysia, Vietnam, Singapore, and in the U.S. have been protesting. In October of 2013, the Madison, Wisconsin City Council unanimously passed a resolution declaring the city to be a "TPP-Free Zone". They saw this trade agreement as "threats to their authority and the job they had been elected to do."[297]

As of 2013, TPP protesters had turned out in mass in Salt Lake City and in Los Angeles, and more than 400 organizations representing 15 million Americans have already petitioned Congress to refuse to allow Fast Track.[298]

Local communities in Oregon are working to remove legal barriers of corporate "rights" and state preemption by passing their own version of a Model Food Bill of Rights. The bill will protect local family firms, ban genetically modified organisms, and ensure the humane treatment of livestock.[299]

---

[295]Ibid.
[296]Ibid.
[297]Newby, David. Madison City Unanimously Passes Resolution Opposing Trans-Pacific Partnership. 30 October. Available @ 2013popularresistance.org.
[298]2013. Hundreds of U.S. Organizations Urge Congress To Replace Fast Track. *Citizens Trade Campaign.* 4 March. Available @ Octobercitizenstrade.org CTC.
[299]Democracy School. Available @ celdf.org/democracy-school

The CELDF Democracy School

This TPP multi-national corporate movement to overrule sovereign governments is now being challenged by American citizens who are establishing their own local legislative authority. The CELDF (Community Environmental legal Defense Fund) was launched in 2013. Its mission statement articulates the right to local self-government and the rights of nature.

Its Community Rights State law Center is a non-profit, public interest law firm providing free and affordable legal services to communities facing threats to their local environment, local agriculture, local economy, and quality of life.[300] It provides model state legislation and state constitutional amendments to people working to expand civil and political rights for their individuals and communities and to elevate those rights above the "rights" currently claimed by corporations and other business entities. It has started engaging with ten states and will add more states as they become active.[301]

Using the same tactics as ALEC which focus their efforts on states to replace public services with private for-profit services, the CELDF is establishing Democracy Schools to teach citizens how to legally strengthen local state governments in order to protect their communities from outside corporate decisions whose only concern is profit!

Their goal is to defend human rights and environmental stability on our planet.

---

[300]Ibid.
[301]Ibid.

CHAPTER SEVEN   TERRORISM

"Terrorists are often compared to cancerous tumors that destroy themselves when they destroy their hosts, but they are actually much more like mobile parasites who live in host bodies but can move from host to host as they infect and destroy the systems off which they live.....”[302]

- Benjamin R. Barber, *Fear's Empire*

Like anti-matter, a virus cannot reproduce itself. It must attach itself to a host cell in order to continue existing. A virus also has the ability to spread and does not respect geographic boundaries.

This is also a description of terrorism. Terrorism can only survive by hijacking populations. Once it does that, it grows and spreads out until it has weakened and destroyed entire societies.

We all know the feeling when we come down with the flu. An attack puts our immune systems to work. While that activity is going on, the rest of our body shuts down and all our energy must be devoted to conquering the virus. Our body cannot engage in providing energy for other activities at the same time that it is fighting this battle because it cannot do both things at once. In other words, we cannot grow creatively or live fully at the same time that our immune system is fighting off a threat.

[302] Barber, Benjamin R. *Fear's Empire: War, Terrorism, and Democracy*, (New York: W.W. Norton & Co. c 2003), p. 117.

This is what terrorism does to a society. Terrorists do some outrageous thing to activate our fear and from that moment on, we no longer feel safe. As Dr. Marsha Sinetar writes in her book, *Ordinary People As Monks And Mystics:*

> "A fearful individual is a person held in check, stunted, even crippled—although his body may be perfectly formed. The longer fear persists, the more he is stuck and frozen..."[303]

Little by little we allow fear to restrict our freedoms, our privacy, our ideals, our ability to be open to others, and our growth. We send our young men and women off to battle, thousands die, many more thousands return with wounded bodies and damaged psyches.

As we increase our military spending and go deeper and deeper into debt, we continue to waste more lives and spend trillions of dollars on a war we can't win. One terrorist act can paralyze a country. Meanwhile, terrorists can sit back and watch how effective was their blow. We cannot finally conquer terrorism through military action alone.

Meanwhile, we can kill ourselves trying.

This war against terror does not discriminate. Like weeds in a garden, the "enemy" is within civilian populations. Any attempt to do battle with terrorism involves harming innocent victims, many of whom are women, young children, and infants (precision-guided missiles notwithstanding). Escalating brutality in the Middle East proves once again that there is no way to win a war on terror through militarism alone. It does nothing but spread by motivating and empowering sleeper cells of hatred all over the world.

This insanity plays out in brutal violence in Afghanistan, Syria, Pakistan, Iraq, Yemen, and in countries in Africa. Yet, it has not brought our world one iota of permanent stability or security. Instead, it has resulted in a weird power game of "musical chairs" in which countries attempt to strategically position themselves.

---

[303]Sinetar, Marsha. *Ordinary People As Monks And Mystics: Lifestyles for Self-discovery,* (New York: 1986), p. 14.

What to do? One never completely gets rid of weeds in a garden by just dropping poisons on them. It requires much more effort than that. You get much better results by also tending to and sweetening the soil, planting good seed, giving it the light, water, and nutrients it needs, thus preventing new weeds from taking hold. Eventually, the good seed takes over.

Loss of Human Protections and Rights

In the goal of fighting terrorism the next step taken is to whittle away at our rights. In his book, *Crossing the Rubicon,* Michael Ruppert explained that not many Americans were aware of the total and complete power that was given to FEMA under the control of Vice President Richard Cheney. It was signed into law just eight months after 9/11.[304]

This may seem odd given the lack of effectiveness FEMA displayed during the Katrina tragedy. Nevertheless, should it appear we are under a severe enough terrorist threat, FEMA has the legal authority to take control over every facet of our society by suspending civil government, our transportation systems, our food, our education, our jobs, and anything else it deems necessary.

Ruppert explained that this would amount to martial law with no Congressional oversight. FEMA would have to answer to no one. It would have the right to legally ignore our Constitution and our Bill of Rights! Another example is the weakening of the Foreign Intelligence Surveillance Act (FISA), which was written after the Watergate scandal to protect citizens from wire-tapping. Since 9/11, immunity was granted to the telecom industry making it possible for our government to collect the metadata on all our phone conversations, internet transactions, and e-mails.

Watching Americans

Now, it is one thing to know God is always watching us but it is quite another to let governments enjoy that privilege! Even before the Edward Snowden

---

[304]Ruppert, Michael C. *Crossing The Rubicon,* (Gabriola Island, B.C.: New Society Publishers, c2004), pp. 414, 415.

exposure, James Bamford, in his April 2012 article in *Wired* magazine, described the NSA's latest heavily-fortified $2 billion center in Bluffdale, Utah—1 million square feet housing data-collecting devices to collect and store "all forms of communication".[305]

And because the NSA will be able to cryptanalyze heavily encrypted computer data of not only foreign users but users in the United States as well, the privacy of all our personal and financial information is in question.[306] It doesn't take a leap of the imagination to realize how all this information can be used against us.

Global Surveillance

As a result of the Patriot Act, here in America not only our right to privacy, but our traditional justice system of innocent until proven guilty has been reversed. In *The Soft Cage,* author Christian Parenti writes: "In the name of fighting terror, cops and the FBI are seeking new powers to keep regular dossiers on anyone, no matter how law-abiding."[307]

And the ACLU is concerned with the potential danger of fusion centers developed across our country that allow state and local police to integrate data collected on us with federal national security data banks.[308]

So, in our passionate quest for security the final achievement of watching everyone has finally arrived. Yet, in spite of the massive amount of dollars spent on all this questionable zeal for our safety, our global security system has failed to anticipate terror attacks.

The world saw how even the most heavily applied surveillance systems of London failed to protect its citizens. The UK may have held the dubious honor of being the most CCTV saturated country in Europe (over "2.5 million cameras).[309] But all this surveillance did not prevent the bombing of London's subways. Neither did French security systems anticipate and prevent the Charlie Hebdo

[305]Banford, James. 2012. Inside the Matrix. *Wired.* April.
[306]Ibid.
[307]Parenti, Christian. *The Soft Cage: Surveillance In America,* (New York: Basic Books, c2003).
[308]Stanley, Jay and Steinhardt, Barry. 2007. Even Bigger, Even Weaker: The Emerging Surveillance Society: Where Are We Now? *American Civil Liberties Union.* September. Available @ aclu.org.
[309]Parenti, Christian. *The Soft Cage: Surveillance In America,* (New York: Basic Books, c2003).

attack in Paris in which 12 people at that satirical magazine were killed. Predictively, an enhancement of fear has infiltrated itself even more into the psyche of that country.

Total Information Awareness

Mobile phones and devices are used by millions of Americans. When they are turned on they are easily located by phone companies. Thanks to Global Positioning System (GPS) chips, this information makes it easy for us to be tracked. In *The Naked Crowd,* author Jeffrey Rosen quotes the words of Senator Maria Cantwell:

> "What I don't think people realize, is that we are just at the tip of
> the iceberg...I try to explain some of the new technology to my
> colleagues...You're going to be able to be driving and say, 'Hey, take
> me to the nearest Starbucks,' and they all think that's great.
> And then I say, 'But it also might be stored in a data base that
> may also be able to track where you were at two o'clock in the
> morning.'"[310]

Not only can our whereabouts be tracked for any time or place, but our activity is also recorded through a process known as data-mining, a tool used by the Total Information Awareness Program which can instantly search the computer world for any and all of citizens' private information.

In commenting on this developing panopticon, in *The Buying of the President,* author Charles Lewis notes how former U.S. representative Bob Barr, a conservative Republican, warned that Total Awareness is much worse than the attempt to use Federal workers as peeping toms.

Because it does not depend on someone entering our homes, it is capable of universal surveillance.[311] Apparently, that day has finally arrived.

---

[310]Rosen, Jeffrey. *The Naked Crowd: Reclaiming Security And Freedom In An Anxious Age,* (New York: Random House, 2004) pp. 139, 140.
[311]Lewis, Charles. *The Buying of the President: Who's Really Bankrolling Bush And His Democratic Challengers—And What They Expect in Return,* (New York: Perennial, c2004), p. 181.

Enter the RFID Chip - The Ultimate in Surveillance

Radio Frequency Identification Chips are tags that are so tiny (they can be imbedded in the dot of the lower case letter i) they can be in just about anything and they do not need batteries. Barry Steinhardt, the Director of the ACLU Technology and Liberty Program, tells us they are remotely read computer chips with miniature antennae that can hold unique identification codes for all manufactured items. He says the ultimate intention is to imbed these chips into every consumer product in the world.[312]

He noted that Wal-Mart already has plans for the implementation of these chips. Steinhardt also explains that these chips can be imbedded into cash, government documents, drivers' licenses, and biometric passports. Hidden readers for these passive tags, which can be read from less than an inch to 20-30 feet to a much longer read range for active (self-powered) tags, can be in floor tiles, carpeting, floor mats, doorways, shelving, and public spaces, etc.[313]

Our world of surveillance has now reached new heights! By linking personal identifiers (like our licenses) with these tags, individuals are tracked without their knowledge or consent. This can be accomplished through a linkup with our existing national data-base system technology.

As time goes on, more and more products will have these RFID chips imbedded in them. Our credit card transactions, real estate records, vehicle registrations, consumer tastes, subscriptions, and anything else you can name, are all in these data bases.

Once more should citizens be concerned? When all our personal information and buying choices as well as where we are at any given moment of time can be easily retrieved from data bases by some authority, we have then entered into a world we may not particularly like.

---

[312]Steinhardt, Barry. 2004. Director of the ACLU Technology and liberty Program. Statement made on RFID Tags Before the Commerce, Trade and Consumer Protection Subcommittee of the House Committee on Energy and Commerce. 14 July. Available @ aclu.org.
[313]Ibid.

Unholy Alliances

Couple this, with final control of a world economy by a one-world powerhouse that has superimposed itself over the laws of separate sovereign governments and we will have lost all our autonomy, privacy, and buying power. We already know what happens when governments and corporations form an unholy alliance; it is called Fascism.

Steinhardt warns: "What is at stake is no less than how and when Americans will be identified and tracked here and around the world."[314]

And now we learn that surveillance is now able to penetrate our walls. FBI and U.S. Marshalls deploy radars that can detect human breathing through walls at a distance of more than 50 feet.[315]

It is eerily reminiscent of the strategic alliance between Nazi Germany and IBM in executing the holocaust.[316] What ever happened to the sacredness of our privacy? This is a perfect example of the diabolical potential of the dark side of cyberspace.

Public Space

How do we feel when we know that drones, cameras or hidden RFID chips are always recording us? Might that not influence our behavior? Surveillance cameras are now even installed in some charter school classrooms.[317] CCTV systems watch our movements in airports, subways, and malls. Just standing still for too long can tag you as a suspicious person.

Apparently, one should keep moving. Face and behavioral recognition which identifies unusual patterns, can tag anything as a suspicious image, and can then be back-dragged to locate a person.[318]

---

[314]Ibid.

[315] 2015. *Free Speech TV, "Democracy Now – The War and Peace Report"*. Headlines. Report: Police in U.S.Using Radars That Can See Through Wall. 21 January. Available @ democracynow.org.

[316]Parenti, Christian. The *Soft Cage: Surveillance in America,* (New York: Basic Books, c2003), p. 83.

[317]propublica.org/article/charter-school-power-broker-turns-public-education-into-private-profits

[318]Jeffrey Rosen. *The Naked Crowd: Reclaiming Security And Freedom In An Anxious Age,* (New York: Random House, 2004), pp. 45, 46.

Extraordinary Rendition

What happened to Maher Arar, the Syrian-born Canadian citizen, who was flown out of the country from Kennedy Airport to Syria where he was held for one year and repeatedly tortured, has happened to many innocent victims of the war on terror.

Denied any legal representation or communication with his family, Maher was beaten with a cable and held for almost a year in an underground cell the size of a grave. The physical and psychological trauma he endured left him with a loss of confidence, increased emotional distance, a victim of discrimination in trying to find employment, and a fear of ever boarding a plane again.

His wife and children were also put on a list of suspected terrorists. Even though the Canadian government found him innocent of all charges and awarded him $10 million in monetary damages, as of 2006, the United States government still refused to remove him or his family from its terrorist watch list.[319]

Many Americans have already had the unpleasant experience of being detained at airports because their name was on a list, the late Senator Edward Kennedy, the "Lion of the Senate", being one of them.[320]

The Many Masks of Evil

We are reminded of evil's uncanny ability to parade as good. Looking to anticipate the next terrorist attack establishes a very dangerous precedent. In this case, the good of our security is the mask hiding the evil of a loss of privacy and freedom. Just as we have a right to the sacredness of our bodies, we have a right to the sacredness of our privacy and our peaceful use of public space. These rights are not to be tampered with no matter how well-meaning the cause. Claiming to protect us by keeping us under a surveillance system whose effectiveness is at best questionable is, in reality, our undoing!

---

[319]2006. Discussion of Program of Extraordinary Rendition. with Maher Arar. *Free Speech TV, "Democracy Now-The War and Peace Report"*. 27 February.

[320]2004. Senator? Terrorist? A Watch List Stops Kennedy at Airport. The New York Times. 20 August.

As ordinary citizens, it behooves us to have another look at all this passion for our security. What are its fruits? If our privacy is threatened, our freedoms get hijacked, and we are ripe for control by some invisible authority, do we really want it? We have a choice between the democratic use of our public space, or a policed environment.

Congress is the body that Americans rely on to supervise and regulate our country. They have made overtures, but they need to hear from us a lot more! Little by little, under the guise of security we are coming closer and closer to losing all our civil liberties! We may have to keep reminding ourselves of the lesson of the frog who when dropped in warm water, put up no struggle until it was too late.

Terrorists Come and Terrorists Go

So often, houses are divided. Take the example of divisions in Shia and Sunni terrorist groups. To name just a few, we have Hezbollah, Hamas, Taliban, Al-Qaeda, Al-Shebab, Boko Haram, Houthies, and ISIS.

Also, in the real world of secret strategic alliances one often discovers that no one's hands are perfectly clean; there is no pure nation. In the 1980s, the United States was on the same side of the Taliban in Afghanistan in their fight against Soviet occupation. Then it was in a war against the Taliban. And now the target is ISIS.

And consider Turkey—a country considered to be an American ally in wanting to see Syria's Bashar al-Assad and ISIS defeated—also wants to defeat the PKK Kurdistan Working Party in Turkey which is fighting ISIS in Syria. So for Turkey, the enemy of its enemy is still not its friend.

Another example is the dual nature of Saudi Arabia—on the one hand, a long-time U. S. economic partner supplying oil to the West, and on the other, financing Wahhabism, the extreme terrorist organization which nurtured al-Qaeda. Like Turkey, Saudi Arabia would also like to see Syria's Bashar al-Assad defeated by ISIS, but does not want al-Qaeda, ISIS, or the Houthies to make Saudi Arabia its next target. So now, both Houthies and Saudi Arabia are competing for Yemen.

Finally, Russia has stepped into this quagmire with the goal of supporting Syria which puts it on an opposite footing with the United States and its allies.

A Description Of Hell

It boggles the mind the way all are engaged in secret strategies pitting themselves against one other. America is supposedly in a war on terrorism, and because of this, its hands are tied when it comes to addressing terrorist atrocities perpetrated by countries whose cooperation it needs. In its goal of preventing the spread of Communism and Terrorism, the United States has involved itself with questionable military coups in countries all over the world. Its own CIA being guilty of torture, thus compromising our ideals as a nation.

This war on terror, has brought us to the edge of a very slippery slope. Our highest ideals, our quality of life, our individual freedoms, our privacy, and good name are in jeopardy. Even our weapons convict us. Torture has been up for debate. Waterboarding seemed effective. And now the greatest refugee movement in history is spilling over into Europe in a desperate attempt to escape the brutal violence and destruction in their home countries.

The Muslim World

Islam, the fastest-growing religion on this planet, is the second most popular faith in the world. In *Standing Alone in Mecca,* author Asra Nomani writes that it has at least two billion worshippers.[321] Unlike we in the West, Muslims have not separated church from state. Their form of government is a theocracy in which instructions of religious leaders carry all the weight. She explains that when they hear anti-Muslim messianic pronouncements by right-wing religious leaders, they interpret it as representative of Western culture.

We know better, but they don't. Nevertheless, these messianic anti-Muslim statements can leave them feeling threatened. Nomani also points out that in the

---

[321]Nomani, Asra Q. *Standing Alone In Mecca: An American Woman's Struggle For The Soul Of Islam,* (San Francisco: 2005), p. 36.

Muslim culture there is a resentment of occupation (there aren't many Western countries that would welcome being occupied either).[322]

The Dark Side Of Religious Zeal

In *Terror and Liberalism,* author Paul Berman writes of Sayyid Qutb, the influential Islamic writer and Sunni scholar of the 1900s whose masterwork was *In the Shade of the Qur'an.*[323] Qutb saw modern life as a miserable alienation from God. His vision was to see the new Islamic system take concrete form in a Muslim country and, eventually, to lead the world.[324] It is easy to see how bin Laden, who resided, not in the rich palaces of Saudi Arabia, but in the cold mountains of Pakistan, was able to appear as a sincere and humble follower of Allah.[325]

However, dogmatic religious and secularist zeal always carries with it the potential of a corresponding dark side. An element of extremism develops and the vulnerable and powerless are easily drawn in. Qutb's writings not only provided the framework of Islamic teachings, but also produced Islamist extremists who have as their goal, through violence and Sharia law, the establishment of a pure Muslim world.

This is where history repeats itself. Following in the tradition of the Communist Revolution or the Nazi youth camps, violent jihadists fuel their resentment of the West's occupations in their lands by indoctrinating others to join their cause. In the name of defending Islam, they are taught to resist and attack the values of the modern Western world, easily drawing in disaffected young men and women who are only too eager to join their ranks.

Along with this insanity of extreme religious fervor, fundamentalist Muslim extremists hate us because U.S. policy in the Muslim world has been violent,

---

[322]Ibid, p. 50.
[323]Berman, Paul. *Terror and Liberalism*, (New York: 2003), pp. 64, 87,101.
[324]Ibid.
[325]Scheuer, Michael. *Imperial Hubris: Why The West Is Losing The War On Terror,* (VA: 2004), pp. 3, 4.

aggressive and oppressive. Our actions, which have so often involved torture and cooperation with brutal governments, have fed that hatred.[326]

The truth is there is no shortage of evil in this conflict—there is plenty enough for both sides to project. Whether terrorism is a clash of civilizations or a passionate zeal of extremist jihads, terrorism is anti-life and we really must deal with it.

One thing is sure—evil does not discriminate. In varying intensities, it is within every human being, many times unknowingly, but in that case, its power is greatly enhanced.

What we aren't aware of can indeed hurt us!

---

[326]Ibid., P. 105.

CHAPTER EIGHT   EVIL

"The doing evil to avoid an evil cannot be good."

\- Coleridge

The Real Enemy

Truly, the real threat to mankind is evil itself—not the carrier.

On the one hand, a photo shows a young Iraqi teenager with both of his arms blown away by a U.S. bomb—he is being carried on a stretcher with his aunt, covered in black, following close behind. On the other hand, televised pictures of terrified western prisoners kneeling before the swords of their insurgent jihadi captors, bring home the same message of evil.

Surely this shows how banal and indiscriminating is evil. What, other than incitement of extreme fear, suffering, mistrust, and hatred, are the fruits of these actions? When enough of us realize this we will have finally turned a corner in our human history.

Evil's Many Faces

Evil wears the face of goodness only too well. Instead of concentrating on how we will conquer evil, we would be wiser to first recognize its potential within our very own selves. It is there, to be sure, because it is simply the other side of the coin of materiality. Spell live backward and you get evil. And to destroy one side of a coin, is to destroy the coin.

Evil is anti-life and anti-hope. However, once begun, it grows exponentially. Think back for a moment on the Watergate scandal. At first it appeared to be just a break-in. But as it unfolded, its reality became far more extensive than anyone could have imagined, involving covert action by government officials   and intelligence agencies. That dark scenario may be useful in understanding the Vietnam War, the two Kennedy assassinations, the Martin Luther King assassination, conflict in the Middle East, the "war on terror", and the "war on drugs". [327]

In *Evil*, author Lance Morrow notes how children, nature, humor, and life itself, offend evil.[328] Unfortunately, the more you live with it, the more you get used to it and that is the danger.

To evil, tolerance must never be tolerated. It thrives on inflamed emotions. Fame gives it special status; Morrow points out that there's nothing like celebrity to dazzle us into temporary blindness.[329] It can display impeccable manners. It can use any good cause—*religion* (the Crusades, extremism, jihad, beheading, stoning a woman under the rule *of* sharia), *safety and security* (gag orders, secret surveillance, torture, data mining), *democracy* (globalization, free trade, economic exploitation) and *justice* (solitary confinement, police brutality, capital punishment, racism, and discrimination)

Evil has always had its home in extremism. The true believer, as author Eric Hoffer knew, can be made to do anything.[330] Once committing us to its mass movement, it can make us most loyal, even to the point of committing torture, murder and suicide.

Some of evil's favorite tools are secrecy oaths and covert operations; separating the elite from common humanity is one of its strategies. It needs to classify information because in a secret environment its creativity is greatly enhanced. And as long as evil is hidden, there is no one to challenge it.

Chapter Eight   Evil

[327]the reader is referred to the books, *The Devil's Chessboard,* by author and journalist, David Talbot and *Enrique's Journey* by Pulitzer Prize winning journalist, Sonia Nazario.
[328]Morrow, Lance. *Evil: An Investigation,* (New York: 2003).
[329]Ibid. p. 189.
[330]Hoffer, Eric. *The True Believer*: Thoughts On The Nature Of Mass Movements, (New York: 1951).

Under the ruse of national security, it has been able to appear through such developments as enhanced torture memos, NSA data mining, gag orders, national security letters, and secrecy oaths that have forced government agents and members of investigative committees to remain silent.

It allows for the worst of which mankind is capable—slavery, barbarism, torture, trafficking, invasion of privacy, cover-ups, and manipulation of events to start wars and weaken nations. Unfortunately, by the time we recognize its fruits; evil has already packed up and gone on to its next project.

Speaking Up

Surely, aggression and cowardice also open a wide door for evil. This may be one of the reasons why Hitler was able to arouse so much lack of compassion for his Jewish victims. Who would dare to speak up? Nazi atrocities were given free reign because of these failures of character.

The need to expose injustice, no matter how fraught with risk, will always be with us. One ordinary person's courage and character is far more important than any country's weapons.

As we have seen, had it not been for General Smedley Darlington Butler's lone voice exposing the attempted coup against President Roosevelt, we might very well be living under a fascist dictator today.

Had it not been for Dr. Jeffrey Wigand's exposure of nicotine's addictive effects, many more smokers would have died from cancer.

Had it not been for Daniel Ellsberg's exposure of the Pentagon Papers, the lies perpetrated on the American public about the Vietnam War might never have been known.

Had it not been for Dr. David Graham's exposure of the attempted cover-up by the FDA and Merck Corporation, the dangerous painkiller, Vioxx, would be causing even more thousands of fatal heart attacks (it had caused between 88,000 and 139,000 heart attacks of which 30 to 40 percent were fatal).[331]

Had it not been for whistle blower, Wendell Potter we might still be ignorant of the health insurance industry tactics to deny coverage.[332]

Had it not been for Franz Gayl and his actions resulting in the replacing of inferior military vehicles with MRAP (Mine-Resistant Ambush Protected) vehicles, many more soldiers in the Iraq war would have been killed and injured.[333]

Had it not been for James Bamford and Edward Snowden, Americans would still be unaware of a national surveillance system constantly watching us.

Another hero and whistle blower is two-star Army General Tony Taguba. Seymour Hersh, reporter for *The New Yorker*, describes how Taguba was brave enough to confront high-level military units about the torture going on at Abu Ghraib. He was ignored many times, and then mocked by the then Secretary of Defense, Donald Rumsfeld. But Taguba did not cave, even though he knew investigating detainee abuse would hurt his career. He had served 32 years in the Army, but this was something he could not tolerate. [334]

War - Evil's Ultimate Destination

Mother Nature never fails to expose war's evil nature. In *Reporting,* author David Remnick includes Amos Oz's description of the battlefield: "Battle consists first and foremost of a horrible stench." This stifling mixture of burning rubber and burning metal and burning human flesh and feces."[335] Even long after wars have ended, evil's fruits remain. In Vietnam, napalm was sprayed on vegetation to remove cover.

---

[331]2005. Scherer, Michael. The Side Effects of Truth. In exposing the deadly threat posed by Vioxx, FDA researcher David Graham was serving the public interest. *Mother Jones.* May/June.
[332]Potter, Wendell. *Deadly spin: an insurance company insider speaks out on how corporate PR is killing health care and deceiving Americans.* (New York: Bloomsbury Press, 2010).

[333]2013. Feeney, Lauren. Whistle Blowers: American Heroes? 26 April. billmoyers.com
[334]www.newyorker.com/magazine/2007/06/25/the-generals-report
[335]Remnick, David. *Reporting, Writings From The New Yorker,* (New York: 2006), p. 363.

In *Gellhorn,* author Caroline Moorehead quotes Martha Gellhorn's experience with napalm victims:

> "Napalm worked…because it was jellied gasoline, and the jelly stuck to the flesh while the gasoline burned. We always get the napalm cases in batches…And there's white phosphorous too and it's worse because it goes on gnawing at flesh like rat's teeth, gnawing at the bone."[336]

Other fruits of war are landmines which kill anyone who accidentally steps on them—most often children who regard them as toys. Hands, arms, and legs are lost. Consider that in Laos:

> "From June 1964 to March 1973, the U.S. dropped at least two million tons of cluster bombs on the small, landlocked Southeast Asian country. That's the equivalent of one planeload every eight minutes, 24 hours a day, for nine years—more than were dropped on Germany and Japan during World War II."[337]

Just think of the profits that inventory turnover represented! Yet, in May of 2008, when representatives of more than 100 governments gathered in Dublin, Ireland for a two week discussion aiming to sign a global treaty ban on the use of cluster bombs, the United States (the largest producer of these weapons) along with Russia, China, Israel, India and Pakistan, did not attend.[338]

Jody Williams, who won the Nobel Peace prize in 1997 for her work with the International Campaign to Ban Landmines, reminds us that:

> "…a treaty, a law, a U.N. resolution non-implemented is fundamentally irrelevant…you have to stay committed to the goal."[339]

Her new challenge is killer robots. She explains that a drone always has a human being who has to push the buttons on a computer in order to release the drone's missiles. But the new development in drone technology is now a killer robot. Depending on how it was programmed, the robot decides on its own who and what to target, making it impossible to know who is accountable.

---

[336]Moorehead, Caroline. *Gellhorn A Twentieth-Century Life,* (New York: 2003), p. 352.
[337]2014. *Free Speech TV, "Democracy Now-The War and Peace Report".*
50 Years After U.S. Launched Secret War on Laos, Unexploded Bombs Still Killing Civilians. 25 June. Discussion with Karen Coates and Jerry Redfern. Available @ democracynow.org
[338]2010. *Free Speech TV, "Democracy Now-The War and Peace Report",*
2 August.
[339]2015. Nobel Peace Prize Laureate Launches Campaign to Stop Killer Robots After Winning Ban on Landmines. democracynow.org 2015/4/27.

She says:

> "You certainly can't bring the drone to trial. ...the U.S., of course, is in the lead of making them and thinks that we should keep the door open to them...in the air, on the land and in the sea... They have a vision of swarms of killer robot planes that can attack the opposition."[340]

Once they are flying, there are no men in the middle to take responsibility. Spider-like drones, equipped with tear gas for crowd control, are now just the beginning of a new profitable industry. In 2013 Williams helped launch the Campaign to Stop Killer Robots. She says within nine months, we were able to force the governments of the world to come together in Geneva and start discussing these weapons.[341]

From Stones to Drones

Evil increases its inventory as we increase our talents and skills. In his 2003 book, *Simpson's World,* John Simpson noted that the AK-47, a favorite weapon in the Middle East, was estimated to have reached a number of 80 million since it was first developed by Michail Kalashnikov.[342]

Consider all the complicated and sophisticated weaponry that has been developed throughout the history of human civilization—from the first stone hurled, to complex nuclear warheads, sarin-tipped rockets, drones, killer robots, and now, cyberwarfare.

Evil as Surprise

It can be very shocking when you recognize evil in apparently "good" people. Those who once lived together peacefully can turn on each other with unspeakable vengeance. John Simpson gives us the shocking picture of even a good Hutu Christian teacher and loving mother in Kigali, Rwanda who turned against her neighbors—including even the families of her first communion students. She

---

[340]Ibid.
[341]Ibid.
[342]Simpson, John. *Simpson's World: Dispatches From The Front Lines,* (New York: 2003), p. 87.

carefully wrote down directions for the Hutu killers, telling them where to go and what weapons to use.[343]

This weird phenomenon has been true not only in the Rwandan massacres, but in the Serbian/Bosnian genocide, in the Darfur genocide, in the Middle East, and in any area that has had a history of ethnic cleansing. Clearly there is much we do not understand about the human psyche and its dark side.

The Collective Unconscious

Jung tells us that there are repressed experiences hidden and stored in the personal unconscious. This storehouse of hidden psychic activity is nevertheless influential. It is interesting that he didn't agree that childhood experiences were the only source of this psychic energy. He saw the past history of the human species as also being very significant.[344]

In *A New Earth*, author Eckhart Tolle refers to this hidden psychic energy as the pain-body, saying that it holds the pain of collective humanity and every baby born has it in his and her psyche.[345] That insight might explain how that Hutu Christian mother turned against her neighbors and how ethnic violence continues from generation to generation.

As students of psychology know, Jung saw four basic archetypes that influence individuals.[346]

The *Persona* is explained as the masks we wear to conform to society.

The *Anima and Animus* correspond to our inward face of male and female.

Then there is the most powerful archetype of all: the *Shadow*. This *Shadow* exerts the strongest influence over an individual as well as the relationship with an individual's own sex. When it is repressed, when it is not recognized, it can erupt in violence.

---

[343]Ibid. p. 77.
[344]Yungblut, John R. *The Gentle Art Of Spiritual Guidance*, (New York:1988).
[345]Tolle, Eckhart. *A New Earth: Awakening to Your Life's Purpose*, (New York: 2006), pp. 142, 143.
[346]Hall, Calvin S. and Nordby, Vernon J. *A Primer of Jungian Psychology*, (New York: 1973).

And yet ironically, like the opposite sides of a coin, this *Shadow*—while having the potential for evil, also has the potential for good. It is the source of spirit and inspiration as well as of natural instinct.

Finally, the fourth archetype is the *Self*. This *Self*, which has always been with the individual, is at the center. It is the harmonizer and uniter of all the archetypes. This *Self* is at the end of the journey, not the beginning. It brings all the opposites into harmony. This is why love has no opposite.

Fear

Fear, once hatched, always has a great potential for evil. The great believer in fear is the ego. This is because until it becomes enlightened, the ego believes it is lacking, separate, and alone. But this is a lie! We are not forged in any ill-cast way and we are never separate and alone. In truth, we are connected to everything. Science now knows nothing in creation is separate or alone—all is related. But until the ego recognizes this fact, it will continue to believe that only in struggling with others, can it survive.

Viewing the Enemy In History

In *Hatred,* author William Gaylin explains that hatred is never rational:

> "To sustain hatred, one cannot simply view the enemy as another
> set of people. The enemy must be evil and a menace to our well-being.
> Wartime requires a rapid demonizing of the enemy in order to justify
> the kind of injury that one must inflict on enemy populations..."[347]

There were the isms—Napoleon Bonaparte's French Imperialism, Lenin and Marx's Anti-Liberalism, Britain's Colonialism, Joseph Stalin's and Chairman Mao's Communism, Franco's Right-Wing Ultra-Catholicism, Adolf Hitler's Nazi National Socialism, Mussolini's and Hirohito's Fascism, as well as the many radical Religious Fundamentalisms, and Western Imperialism.

---

[347]Gaylin, Willard, MD. *Hatred: The Psychological Descent into Violence,* (New York: 2003), p.186.

These "isms" foster division, fear, isolation, destruction, and finally, war. Most have also passed into oblivion. Yet, their fruits have lived on in a legacy of unspeakable suffering and death for untold billions on our planet.

Out of curiosity, if you look up the statistics of just a few of the battles and ethnic cleansings of the late 20th and early 21st century (excluding the two World Wars) this is what you find:

Korean War
1950-1953 – 2.8 million killed.[348]

Vietnam War
1965-1975 - Over 3 million killed.[349]

Cambodia
1975 - 1979 – 1 million murdered by the Khmer Rouge. [350]

Iran/Iraq War
1980-1988 - 1 million killed.[351]
Kurds (1988 - Between 100, 000 and 200,000 killed by chemical weapons.)[352]

Tajikistan
1992, 1993 - 50,000 killed.[353]

First Gulf War
1991 - 200,000 Iraqis killed.[354]
Tens of thousands of U.S. soldiers with "Gulf War Syndrome".

Bosnian Civil War
1992 -1995 - 95,535 killed.[355]

---

[348]http://en.wikipedia.org/wiki/Mass_deaths_and_atrocities_of_the_twentieth_century

[349]Gaylin, Willard, M.D. *Hatred: The Psychological Descent into Violence,* (New York: 2003), p. 186.

[350]http://en.wikipedia.org/wiki/Mass_deaths_and_atrocities_of_the_twentieth_century

[351]Berman, Paul. *Terror and Liberalism,* (New York: 2003), p. 108.

[352]Gold, Dore. *Tower of Babble, How The United Nations Has Fueled Global Chaos,* (New York: 2004), p.115.

[353]Gold, Dore. *Hatred's Kingdom: How Saudi Arabia Supports the New Global Terrorism,* (Washington, DC: 2003), p. 135.

[354]Roy, Arundhati. *An Ordinary Person's Guide to Empire,* (Cambridge, Massachusetts: 2004), p. 31.

[355]en.wikipedia.org.//Bosnian _Civil War. *Wikipedia, The Free Encyclopedia,*

Sudan
1990s - between 1.5 and 2 million people killed.[356]

Rwanda
1994 - 800,000 Tutsis murdered.[357]

Darfur
2003 – 2004 - Hundreds of thousands killed by Arab Janjaweed.[358]

Sierra Leone
1991 - 1996 - 50,000 people killed.[359]
5 million forced into exile and refugee camps.

Congo
2001 – 2.5 million people killed. [360]

Yugoslavia
1990s - 200,000 people killed. [361]

Afghanistan
1979 - 2004 - 1.5 million killed.. [362]

Iraq War
As of 6/19/07 –1,033,000 killed.[363]

And war is not cheap!

According to a Congressional Research Service, initially in late 2002, the Iraq War was estimated to cost $60 billion and by 2008 this amount had increased to

---

[356]Berman, Paul. *Terror and Liberalism*, (New York: 2003), p. 113.

[357]Hirsh, Michael. *At War With Ourselves: Why America Is Squandering Its Chance To Build A Better World*, (New York: 2003), p. 173.

[358]Human Rights Watch, Sudan. Events of 2004. July 2004. http://www.hrw.org/world-report-2005/sudan

[359]Gold, Dore. *Tower of Babble, How The United Nations Has Fueled Global Chaos*, (New York: 2004), p. 19.

[360]Ibid, p. 20.

[361]Berman, Paul. *Terror and Liberalism*, (New York: 2003), p. 166.

[362]Scheuer, Michael. *Imperial Hubris: Why The West Is Losing The War On Terror*, (VA: 2004), p. 27.

[363]enwikipedia.org/wiki/2003_invasion_of_Iraq_casualties.org. Opinion Research Business (ORB) poll. As of August, 2007.

$648 billion.[364] But it didn't stop there, that cost had finally increased to trillions of dollars—money that went from American taxpayers' pockets into the pockets of multi-national war profiteers.

Wars have put a massive amount of negative energy into the collective unconscious soul (pain-body) of mankind. And in order to keep existing, like a virus, all that negative energy has to continually feed itself on our thoughts. It is no wonder that violence on our planet persists.

WWI and WWII

To get an even clearer picture of where we are headed, the two wars not included in the above list were the two World Wars of the 20th century. What becomes obvious as one looks at these statistics was the sinister buildup of hostilities before and between those two world wars. For example, the Napoleonic Wars had up to 6.5 million deaths[365] and the Russian Civil Wars had 15 million deaths.[366]

And because all that negative energy didn't just disappear, these hostilities made a significant contribution to the two World Wars. But instead of being the war to end all wars, the Great War only ushered in World War II, which was a 600% increase from World War I—from 8 million deaths to over 48 million deaths.[367] Taken together both of these World Wars added up to a cost of $4.353 trillion.[368]

Using Logic

If the goal of wars is to end evil and usher in peace, we should be the most peaceful planet in the universe by now. But we're not. Only this time, our weapons threaten to wipe us out completely!

---

[364]2008. *Associated Press*, Christine Simmons, Congressional Research Service Report. 25 July.
[365]en.wikipedia.org/wiki/Napoleonic_Wars_casualties, *Wikipedia, The Free Encyclopedia.*
[366]www.geocities.com/dtmcbride/hist/wars.html
[367]http:users.cybercity.dk/~dko12530/ww1.htm and warchronicle.com/numbers/WWII/deaths.htm
[368]2008. *Associated Press*, Christine Simmons, Congressional Research Service Report, Christine Simmons. 26 July.

It is clear where this is heading. Once those nuclear warheads start flying, it will be too late. And now, with the new threat of cyberwarfare, we have the potential of destroying any country's economy and infrastructure.

Failure to realize that we are all connected, that no one is immune from the physical and psychological results of human violence inflicted anywhere on our planet, is evil's ultimate success and humanity's ultimate failure. All that results is a growing amount of invisible negative energy waiting to explode again on our planet along with a growing number of war profiteers only too eager to pocket their profits.

And explode it will, since our weapons have become much more sophisticated and deadly. Surely, if we are so unwise as to let this happen, a third world war could take with it most of the inhabitants of our earth. And the real unlucky ones would be the survivors.

An Illness Of Childhood?

In *Cosmos*, author Carl Sagan, wrote:

> "Microbiologists and physicians study diseases mainly to cure people. Rarely are they rooting for the pathogen. Let us study war as if it were, as Einstein aptly called it, an illness of childhood.
>
> We have reached the point where proliferation of nuclear arms and resistance to nuclear disarmament threaten every person on the planet….We, nuclear hostages—all the peoples of the Earth—must educate ourselves about conventional and nuclear warfare. Then we must educate our governments."[369]

War's Backers

We might start by asking who financially benefits from war? Chemical and weapons manufacturers, oil companies, construction and engineering contractors, drug and sex traffickers, security and surveillance industries, corporate mercenary armies, and corrupt leaders profit handsomely. The more wars that occur, the greater is their inventory turnover!

---

[369]Sagan, Carl. *Cosmos,* (New York: 1980), p. 330.

Not to be pedantic, but isn't this belief in the success of warfare a bit outworn? Surely, there have been enough attempts at it throughout our history. Yet, where has all of this killing gotten us?

How much mistrust, misery, bitterness and hatred has been fueled by these wars—bitterness and hatreds that continue with each new generation? How much have our natural resources been wasted? How horrifically has our environment been compromised and our human needs neglected? If war is truly the only way to resolve our problems, then we are already doomed!

We can argue that sometimes we must fight in a war as was the case of World War II. Yes, we did ultimately have to resort to violence, and those who sacrificed their lives deserve our honor and respect. But we surely can see that events leading up to that war reflected the fears, bitterness, greed, lust for power, prejudice, mistrust, and lack of wisdom—in other words--the unenlightened ego, existing in the minds of humanity.

And we can surely see that the fruits of that war have launched us into this present nuclear age along with a Middle East whose arbitrarily redrawn boundaries promise to bring about even more future conflict. Might it not be time to finally step outside the box and look for a better alternative? All those unfortunate enough to remain alive after the last violent act is perpetrated on this planet will have learned this lesson well.

Meanwhile, we know we should do better than this. The truth is there is no final war to end all wars. There may be short-term victories, but there is always another bigger battle waiting to be fought, more humans to be killed, more war profiteers to increase their wealth, power, and control over our planet, and more negative energy stored in humanity's collective unconscious.

Even our physical bodies show us how life can either thrive or defend, but it cannot do both at the same time. Guns and bombs are instruments of death. And in death, life loses, civilizations are destroyed, and evolution is thwarted. Is there no hope for a better destiny for humanity other than destruction for us and for our planet?

PART II

INTRODUCTION

At this stage of our evolution, wisdom is challenging us to recognize and let go of our old failing beliefs in separation. She is giving us a last chance— to continue on in the same path of destruction, or to realize how connected we all are to each other and to all life on our planet.   In truth, we are so intertwined with everything in the universe that to abuse others, is to abuse our very own selves as well.

Our thoughts which just like the force of gravity which cannot be seen yet are just as powerful, always draw like-minded energy to us. And just as energy and gravity exist, a zero field of unity consciousness also exists.

Though it cannot be seen, this zero field is all around us. Its field of operation is in us as well as outside of us. It experiences its creation through us and has always been urging us forward to achieve our destiny as evolving spiritual human beings. And because it respects our dignity and freedom, it does not use force—it lets us choose life or death.

Knowing this, how sane is it to entertain life-destroying thoughts that elicit emotions of fear and anxiety. Just as the cell membrane stands guard over our cells to control what is allowed in, we can learn to stand guard over our mind to control which thoughts we allow to influence our actions.

CHAPTER NINE   EXTREMISM VS. COMPASSION

"Our prayers for others ought never to be: "God! give them the light Thou has given to me! But: Give them all the light and truth they need for their highest development."

Gandhi

God— Judge, Lover, or Both?

Is God to be feared, or is God to be loved? One thing is for sure; you can't do both at the same time. What parent would feel joy at receiving the love of one's children if it was fearfully forced upon them? And as President Franklin D. Roosevelt wisely said, "The only thing to fear is fear itself."

Fearing God starts with a religious training in childhood. The male is at the top, just under God, with everyone else below him. These systems have put nature, women, and the body at the bottom of the pecking order.

And loving a concept can be pretty difficult. We are still left unsatisfied, confused, and disappointed. Truth be told, we really don't want someone else's handed down faith. We want to feel it coming from our own unique self, and unless we can actually fall in love with our creator, we really are not satisfied with someone else's version. We can have a hard time loving ourselves, for heaven's sake. And as for trusting God, well, if God is to be trusted, why do all those bad things happen?

So we search. We listen to all the voices out there that would give us answers. The plurality of religions on this planet is evidence of that search. It is no wonder there has never been a successful one-world religion. The best we can do is use what we feel in our own personal experiences; we certainly don't appreciate being force-fed someone else's.

But however we describe it, this mystery of God is just that—a mystery. No one has exclusive knowledge of God. Yet, we do have reflections of God in the teachings and lives of the spiritual masters who have walked our earth. The operative words here are teachings and lives—not the dogma which followed them.

Taking God Outside Of The Box

What if we did see God differently? What if God is so connected to us, we could never cut ourselves off? What if we could actually trust that God loves us with all our imperfections? Could we trust a God like that?

Actually, nothing less than falling in love with our creator is what humanity longs to experience. But we cannot be fooled. threatened, manipulated, bribed, or tricked into it. No well-traveled rut will do. Preachers can shout till they are blue in the face that we will burn in hell if we don't accept their God, but still we will not have surrendered our hearts.

Just as you cannot eat or sleep for anyone, the journey of the soul must be experienced by each person individually. This is why we were told that we must each be born again in spirit.

Our Unique Soul

Have you ever tried to relate a moving personal experience to someone, using just words? Even great authors and poets find this challenging. Words fail us at times like that. To hear a piece of music is a world away from just looking at the notes on a sheet. We must have the experience! We must feel and that is what our soul does; it feels. This soul of ours is always speaking to us through our feelings. It is not through our intellect that our spirit speaks to us, it is through our feelings.

Sin as Disconnection

Do we expect our children to be perfect? When they are not, do we smite them or condemn them to torture, or death? If we never made poor judgments, how would we grow in wisdom? Is this not one of the ways we grow? The tragedy of sin is in being estranged, becoming cut off, losing our joy and compassion. We reap what we sow, yes, but we can turn around at any time. Not to save ourselves from eternal damnation, but to save ourselves from the living hell of disconnection while we yet live.

This disconnection is first from ourselves. We turn around to connect with ourselves once again. We may think we have severed our connection to God, but God never severs the divine connection with us.

Old and New Wineskins

This new millennium is challenging each of us to make a choice between two roads. On one road, life is a competition for survival, wealth, status, and control.

However, as this new millennium dawns, a second road is beckoning us. It is traveled by those who search for spiritual truth from within their own hearts. Those who embark on this journey have learned to rely on their God-given abilities to discriminate the wheat from the chaff. "By their fruits ye shall know them" (Matt 7.20),[370] is their guide.

In letting go of the heavy burdens of religious control and traditional authority these people are stepping into unchartered territory. For many, it is a slow, follow-your light process and the beacon must be one's own inner voice of truth.

Chapter Nine   Dogma Vs. Compassion

[370] Authorized King James Version.

But these are not anarchists, nor are they warmongers—they know that human life is too precious. They know that to use violence to solve a conflict only increases violence and conflict. They are coming to realize that matter and spirit are completely entangled—that they exist on a living, breathing planet in which they are no more separate from its life than they are separate from their own body cells.

Of course, they recognize evil, not just in others, but also in themselves--they recognize the existence of their own dark shadow. Having faced down their own dragons they very graciously allow the rest of us to do the same in our own time and in our own way. They have understood the meaning of:

> "...cast out first the beam out of thine own eye, and then shalt thou see clearly to pull out the mote that is in thy brother's eye." (Luke 6:42)[371]

They don't believe that heaven can only be found somewhere after they die. They believe that it is just waiting patiently to be allowed full reign in each one of us while we yet live!

Those who realize their own unique self-worth are not threatened by the uniqueness and talents of others. As Carol Burnett always attributed her phenomenal success to simply allowing others to be funny too, they know each person has a unique contribution to make because each person is as unique and equally important to the whole as are the pieces of a puzzle or the spokes on a wheel.

---

[371] Authorized King James Version.

CHAPTER TEN   WISDOM

"A vision that makes you choose fixed sides isn't a vision."[372]
Deepak Chopra, *Peace Is The Way*

By outwitting anti-matter at the beginning of cellular life, wisdom has brought us to this present stage of our evolution. Wisdom has cleverly accomplished this by turning simple life into more and more complex forms of biology.

And now the ball is in *our* court. The time has come to change the game. Quantum mechanics has already laid out the ground work for us. It shows us that the old bugaboo—separation—is just an illusion. Schroeder tells us that all particles, regardless of where they are in the universe, are instantly aware of each other, and they all have an effect on each other. This phenomenon sometimes referred to as the zero field of consciousness, is one of science's most significant discoveries.

The truth is we are all connected, and the way we treat others always reflects back to us. We are not insulated from the results of vengeance, jealousy, greed, violence, and environmental damage any more than the air we breathe is not insulated from the pollutants we put into it. An eye for an eye and a tooth for a tooth is the modus operandi of a primitive world destined to self-destruct. The wise know this. They know forgiveness is a gift one makes to one's self because

---

Chapter Ten   Wisdom

[372]Chopra. Deepak. *Peace Is The Way: Bringing War And Violence To An End,* (New York: 2005), p. 138.

to keep irritating an old wound prevents it from healing. Until we learn to recognize when our actions are motivated by negativity, we will continue to condemn our species to evolutionary failure.

If it is true, that what is outside of us always mirrors what is inside of us, then it is time to bite the bullet, as they say, and take a good hard look at our thoughts and attitudes—at the log in our own eye before projecting judgment onto others. After all, as Jung reminds us, we can't be whole until we do.

Who Will Inherit The Earth?

It really *will* be the meek because they will be the only ones who will respect it. The meek will put a priority on wisdom, compassion, life, joy, tolerance, cooperation and creativity. They will look at the fruits of a vision—never just its intention! These are the ones Carl Sagan referred to when he wrote:

> "For we are the local embodiment of a Cosmos grown to self awareness. We have begun to contemplate our origins: starstuff pondering the stars; organized assemblages of ten billion billion billion atoms considering the evolution of atoms; tracing the long journey by which, here at least, consciousness arose.
>
> Our loyalties are to the species and the planet. We speak for Earth. Our obligation to survive is owed not just to ourselves but also to that Cosmos, ancient and vast, from which we spring."[373]

To see the fruits of *unbridled capitalism*, they will see colonialism, the private takeover of public institutions, deregulation, pollution, child labor, income inequality, corrupted governments, global warming, mass surveillance, and compromised ecological systems.

To see the fruits of *racism*, they will see abusive prison systems, ignorance, red lining, poverty, human injustice, prejudice, intolerance, and violence.

---

[373]Sagan, Carl. *Cosmos.*(New York: 1980). P. 345

To see the fruits of *warfare,* they will see demolished cities, mass refugee dislocations, drug and sex trafficking, failed states, a military industrial complex with its weapons of biological, chemical, and nuclear weapons, killer drones, and cyber warfare.

To see the fruits of *authoritarian religion*, they will see atheism, prejudice, discrimination, fear, intolerance, misogyny, sexual abuse, sharia, and patriarchy.

OUR FUTURE, OUR PLANET, AND US

CHAPTER ELEVEN   VISIONS OF CONNECTION

"What I experienced during that three-day trip home was nothing short of an overwhelming sense of universal connectedness...It occurred to me that the molecules of my body and the molecules of the spacecraft were manufactured long ago in the furnace of one of the ancient stars that burned in the heavens about me.

And there was the sense that our presence as space travelers, and the existence of the universe itself, was not accidental but that there was an intelligent process at work. I perceived the universe as in some way conscious."[374]

Dr. Edgar Mitchell, *The Way Of The Explorer*

Third Rock From the Sun

Astronomers speak of plasma in space from which atoms and molecules are formed. What has in the past been considered to be esoteric fable is now discovered to be reality; we do have an informed universe. To realize that we are actually down there on our planet's surface, while at the same time we are able to see its image from above is to begin to get just the tiniest hint of this connection; we are so miniscule a spec on its surface and yet we can be aware of the whole of it. Consciousness opens us up to both places.

Chapter 11   Visions of Connection

[374]Mitchell, Edgar, Dr. *The Way Of The Explorer: An Apollo Astronaut's Journey Through the Material and Mystical Worlds,* (New York: 1996), pp. 3, 4.

The Akashic Record—Fable or Reality?

Ervin Laszlo refers to the A-field as the holographic memory of the universe.[375] Even the farthest distances do not separate us and everything that happens, even our every thought, is somehow recorded in this conscious universal field. What scientists refer to as the A-field, Carl Jung referred to as the collective unconscious. The Jesuit priest and paleontologist, Teilhard de Chardin, saw this phenomenon as consciousness increasing in complexity as an organism increased in complexity. His concept of the evolution of mankind was as a constant attraction to more and more of this consciousness and complexity.[376]

Nonlocality

Scientists are aware of nonlocality—we may be close together, or as far apart as in a distant galaxy, yet we are still all connected. Space allows for immediate linkage and interaction. Adam Rutherford writes:

> "Each movement: every heartbeat, thought, and emotion you've ever had; every feeling of love or hatred, boredom, excitement, pain, frustration, or joy; every time you've been drunk and then hungover; every bruise, sneeze, itch, or snotty nose; every single thing you've ever heard, seen, smelled, or tasted is your cells communicating with one another and the rest of the universe."[377]

Life in the Cosmos

Existence on our planet has evolved from physical (inorganic) to physical-biological (organic) to physical-biological-psychological (the unenlightened ego separate self) and, finally to a physical-biological-psychological-spiritual (unity-enlightened consciousness). And the amazing thing is that the great invisible wisdom that has been responsible for all this is the same great invisible wisdom within each and every one of us.

---

[375]Laszlo, Ervin. *Science and the Akashic Field: An Integral Theory of Everything*, (Rochester, VT: 2004), p. 56.
[376]Yungblut, John R. *The Gentle Art of Spiritual Guidance*, (Warwick, NY: 1988) pp. 64, 65, 68.
[377]Rutherford, Adam. *Creation: How Science is Reinventing Life Itself* (New York, NY: 10014) p. 12.

126

Back to Eden

Human evolution can be seen as the journey from separate self-conscious awareness followed by a conscious awareness of connection with our natural environment and all of humanity. To some, the vision of an earthly garden paradise would seem to be a fantasy entertained only by fools. But is this vision really unattainable?

Faith tells us it has always been within our grasp—birds still sing, brave little crocuses pop up through the snow every spring, and children will always be inspired by fairy tales. The 20th century, in spite of all its violence, has nevertheless planted the seeds toward equality and the joy of connections.

One by one, the barriers of injustice and discrimination are falling. Civil rights, protection of children, workers' rights, women's rights, gay and transgender rights, prison reform, the wisdom and dignity of old age, and a striving toward social justice have all established themselves on our planet.

Our planet has certainly produced its life-affirming visionaries. Included in these ranks are spiritual giants, poets, saints, mystics, artists, educators, composers, scientists, authors, journalists, philosophers, ecologists and freedom leaders. Some of these men and women have made their contributions in the past, and some are with us today. Though not all have been in total agreement, they nevertheless manifest, in their own unique ways, a light on our human condition.

Spiritual Transformation

Evolutionary progress will come only from our very own hearts, and in our very own way, one at a time. Each of us will have to recognize our own shadow before we can reach that Kingdom of Heaven residing within us. Thich Nhat Hanh, the Buddhist peace activist who has brought Palestinians and Israelis together in dialogue, says we are not to try to remove our negative emotions, but instead, "to handle them peacefully by just being mindful of them."[378]

---

[378]Nhat Hanh, Thich. *Peace Begins Here*, (Berkeley: 2004).

Just recognizing them is enough. We must embrace them as tenderly as we would a baby. We are not called to remove our eye; we are called to remove the log within it—and to do it with compassion and care!

True Leadership

In commenting on compassion, Dr. Ronald A. Heifetz, in his book, *Leadership Without Easy Answers,* says that compassion is tough but not abusive.[379] He says it involves leadership in facing the difficult things we would rather avoid. "The respect required in leadership is often the limit-setting love that gives people little leeway for turning their eyes from difficult work. But toughness is not the same thing as the gleeful abuse of power, or vengeful delight."[380]

Mindfulness

We are reminded that compassion, which is mindfulness, is needed; first for ourselves, then for others. And what is mindfulness?

Buddhism speaks of 51 categories of seeds. Which seeds are watered is up to each individual. Mindfulness is simply not watering the wrong seeds. The question is not is the Kingdom of God available here and now, because, of course, like fish in the ocean, we have always existed in the Kingdom. The real question is, are we available to the Kingdom? Accepting forgiveness and compassion, first for ourselves, and then for others opens that door.

Deepak Chopra compares this urge towards spiritual transformation to that of a two-year old becoming a three year-old.[381] It just happens naturally. He says wonder, art, beauty, joy, adventure, laughter, play, kindness, truth, non-judgment and physical connection are what children thrive on. This is how nature works. It

---

[379]Heifetz, Ronald A. *Leadership Without Easy Answers,*(London: 1994), p. 243.

[380]Ibid.

[381]Chopra, Deepak. *Peace is the Way: Bringing War And Violence To An End*, (New York: 2005), pp.140, 141.

is also how spiritual evolution works. New desires propel us. We do not have to manufacture them, they just happen.

Shalom

In *The God We Never Knew,* Borg compares the heart to an egg which must hatch. In order for this to happen, he says the shell (the separate ego) must break.[382] This egg (our heart) may hatch through life experiences of grief, spontaneous joy, despair, or the wisdom of age. He speaks of *shalom* as a vision for all of humanity. Much more than just peace, *shalom* means well-being and freedom from every kind of negativity.[383]

---

[382]Borg, Marcus J. *The God We Never Knew: Beyond Dogmatic Religion to a More Authentic Contemporary Faith,* San Francisco: 1997), p. 114.

[383]Ibid., p. 133.

CONCLUSION

The earth recognizes people in whom God flowers. There is a
sensuousness, a centeredness, a grace to their movement. ...They
are the magical people for whom the earth has longed. "[384]

Ken Carey, *Starseed*

The Fruits of Wisdom

This book began with noting how the physicist, Gerald Schroeder, speaks of the *Neshama* as the soul of humanity—it began with the creation and has been with us ever since. He says this intelligence looks at whatever picture our brain paints and knows if that choice will bring us closer to the unity that pervades all existence.

But, it will also always let us make our own choices and reap the fruits of those choices. To continue believing that we are all separate from one another and isolated from the fruits of our actions will surely bring us to a tragic end. Our planet, our lives, and the lives of our children depend on our finally realizing that whatever we do to the least of us, we do to all of us.

"Except a man be born again, he cannot see the kingdom of God" (John 3.3).[385] These are not just empty words. They obviously mean that there is a kingdom of God to be seen—not just after we die—but right here and now on our earth. Jung described this spiritual rebirth as the harmonizing of all archetypes into the Self which is the great unifier and which has no opposite. We have a choice – we can

---

Conclusion

[384]Carey, Ken. Starseed: The Third Millenium, (New York: 1991), p. 98.
[385]Authorized version of King James Bible.

continue in the same way, arming ourselves against each other and plundering our planet until we finally self-destruct, or we can finally realize that we are all connected, and how we treat others and our planet will ultimately decide our fate.

If we wisely choose life over death we will actually begin to reduce that accumulated *pain body* that exists in the universal unconscious of humanity. And like the phenomenon of the "hundredth monkey" effect, once a critical mass is reached, a peaceful species of mankind with new beliefs and new behaviors will finally be able to spread across our planet—and the healing will begin.

www.ingramcontent.com/pod-product-compliance
Lightning Source LLC
Chambersburg PA
CBHW050453290526
45786CB00006B/2273